PENGUIN BOOKS
¡Floricanto Sí!

BRYCE MILLIGAN is the literature program director
of the Guadalupe Cultural Arts Center, one of the
largest and oldest Latino arts centers in the United
States. He is the author of several books for young
adults and three volumes of poetry.

MARY GUERRERO MILLIGAN is a school librarian
and Children's Book Editor for Corona Publishing of
San Antonio, Texas.

ANGELA DE HOYOS is an internationally known
poet and the publisher of M&A Editions, a small Chi-
cano press.

Together, Bryce Milligan, Mary Guerrero Milligan,
and Angela de Hoyos were editors of *Daughters of the
Fifth Sun: A Collection of Latina Fiction and Poetry*
(1995).

¡*Floricanto Sí!*

A Collection of Latina Poetry

Edited by

BRYCE MILLIGAN
MARY GUERRERO MILLIGAN
ANGELA DE HOYOS

PENGUIN BOOKS

PENGUIN BOOKS

Published by the Penguin Group
Penguin Putnam Inc., 375 Hudson Street,
New York, New York 10014, U.S.A.
Penguin Books Ltd, 27 Wrights Lane,
London W8 5TZ, England
Penguin Books Australia Ltd, Ringwood,
Victoria, Australia
Penguin Books Canada Ltd, 10 Alcorn Avenue,
Toronto, Ontario, Canada M4V 3B2
Penguin Books (N.Z.) Ltd, 182–190 Wairau Road,
Auckland 10, New Zealand

Penguin Books Ltd, Registered Offices:
Harmondsworth, Middlesex, England

First published in Penguin Books 1998

10 9 8 7 6 5 4 3 2 1

LIBRARY OF CONGRESS CATALOGING-IN-PUBLICATION DATA
¡Floricanto sí! : a collection of Latina poetry / edited by Bryce
Milligan, Mary Guerrero Milligan, Angela De Hoyos.
        p.   cm.
    ISBN 0 14 058.893 0
    1. American poetry—Hispanic American authors.
2. Hispanic American women—Poetry.   3. American
poetry—20th century.   4. Hispanic Americans—Poetry.
I. Milligan, Bryce, 1953–   .   II. Milligan, Mary Guerrero.
III. De Hoyos, Angela.
PS591.H58F58   1998
811'.54080868—dc21   97-34445

Printed in the United States of America
Set in Goudy
Designed by Helene Berinsky

This volume is dedicated to the
GUADALUPE CULTURAL ARTS CENTER
San Antonio, Tejas

una luz en las tinieblas
para todas las Latinas en todos lares

☙ ☙ ☙

¿Pies para qué los quiero
si tengo alas pa' volar?

Why do I need feet
when I have wings to fly?
—FRIDA KAHLO

ACKNOWLEDGMENTS

❧ The editors of this volume wish to acknowledge with gratitude the work of all those Latina editors and anthologists who preceded us: Estela Portillo Trambley for opening the door with her 1973 Latina issue of *El Grito*; Evangelina Vigil-Piñon for the "Woman of Her Word" issue of *Revista Chicano-Riqueña*; Lorna Dee Cervantes for her early work with Mango Press; Norma Alarcón for creating and maintaining Third Woman Press; Gloria Vando for her innovative *Helicon 9*; Gloria Anzaldúa and Cherríe Moraga for their groundbreaking anthology *This Bridge Called My Back: Writings by Women of Color*; Tey Diana Rebolledo and Eliana S. Rivero for their *Infinite Divisions: An Anthology of Chicana Literature*; Carla Trujillo for her *Chicana Lesbians: The Girls Our Mothers Warned Us About*; Roberta Fernández for her *In Other Words: Literature by Latinas of the United States*, and Lillian Castillo-Speed for her *Latina: Women's Voices from the Borderlands*—not to mention all the activist critics/scholars/editors like Marcella Aguilar-Henson, Norma E. Cantú, Martha Cotera, Inés Hernández-Avila, María Herrera-Sobek, Carolina Hospital, Juanita Luna Lawhn, Naomi Lindstrom, Delia Poey, Naomi Quiñónez, Sonia Saldivar-Hull, Rosaura Sánchez, and Bernice Zamora. These women—and dozens of others—struggled against tremendous odds over the past two decades to bring the poetry and fiction of Latina writers into the awareness of readers and scholars around the world. Without the often valiant efforts of these women, Latina literature would surely not be recognized, as it is today, as being one of the most vibrant and interesting branches of contemporary American writing.

Credit is also due to one New York agent in particular, Susan Bergholz, and to those few editors at the major American publishing houses, including Julie Grau at Riverhead/Putnam, John Glusman at Farrar, Straus and Giroux, Joanne Wyckoff at Ballantine, Rosemary Ahern at Plume, Shannon Ravennel at Algonquin, and Gerry Howard at Norton, who have had the vision and tenacity to shepherd such Latina luminaries as Julia Alvarez, Ana Castillo, Lisa Chávez, and Sandra Cisneros into international awareness. We are especially pleased to thank our editor at Penguin, Kristine Puopolo, and Penguin publisher Kathryn Court for their support and hard work on the volume in hand.

Likewise, a few other males deserve mention for their roles as publishers, scholars, and teachers, whose generous support of the careers of Latina writers over the years has had a significant impact on the field. Among others, we are especially grateful to Rudolfo Anaya, José Armas, Juan Bruce-Novoa, Jim Cody, Rolando Hinojosa, Nicolás Kanellos, Gary Keller, José Limón, Francisco Lomelí, José Montoya, Julian Olivares, José Flores Peregrino, Juan Rodríguez, Jim Sagel, Gary Soto, Charles Tatum, Luis Alberto Urrea, and Tino Villanueva. *Todos hombres con alma.*

On a more personal level, we wish to thank Moises Sandoval, both for his twenty-plus years of support for Latina writers as the generous printer/publisher (with Angela de Hoyos) of M&A Editions, and for the uncounted hours spent at his computer and scanner preparing the manuscript of this volume. *¡Mil gracias, Moises!* We couldn't do it without you.

CONTENTS

INTRODUCTION

The way slivers of light shift and are sifted
through narrow gaps in tropical leaves,
just so, a young woman's life is winnowed:
her love, her future separated

from her past, as if one were light and one
shadow . . .

—ROSEMARY CATACALOS,
"A Silk Blouse"

The term "floricanto," which literally translates as flower-and-song, is the Spanish equivalent of the Nahuatl compound meaning poetry (*in xochitl in cuicatl*, or *xochicuicatl*). It is a word laden with powerful mythic, aesthetic, and political associations, both ancient and modern. Cuahtencoztli, an Aztec philosopher with a penchant for what is generally termed Socratic dialogue, once asked, "How is truth best spoken?" He was answered by Prince Tecayehuatzin, who claimed "Only poetry—*xochicuicatl*—can express truth." The prince's assertion was not disputed. In fact, scholars have come to believe that this connection between truth and poetry was an elemental tenet of the Aztec world view.

Some seven hundred years later, the term resurfaced. Chicano writers, inspired by the poet Alurista's 1969 call for the reestablishment of Aztlán, the mythical homeland of the ancient Aztecs, began looking for a name for the first Chicano literary festival. Festival Floricanto: A National Chicano Literature Symposium was held at the University of Southern California's

Chicano Studies Center in 1973. Subsequent to that conference, an anthology appeared, *Festival de Flor y Canto*, a title that evoked both the Nahuatl word and, playfully, the contemporary hip culture of California. More festivals and more anthologies followed under similar titles. Before long, "floricanto" had become the term of choice for any Chicano literary gathering.

"¡*Floricanto Sí!*" is an affirmative declaration of the value of poetry as an active force in our lives—a force that brings people together to celebrate *la palabra y la cultura*, the word and the culture. If *floricanto* has its roots in Nahuatl, *sí* is pure Spanish; thus the title is itself mestiza in nature. Although we have selected a title with its roots in Mexico, the work itself embraces Latinas of many national origins. We offer this work in the spirit of those early gatherings, which celebrated a suppressed culture through the beauty and insights of poetry. Echoing Tecayehuatzin, we believe that poetry—*xochicuicatl*—lies at the heart of the Latina's way of seeing the world.

Although it was fiction that finally attracted national attention (in the early 1990s) to Latina writers like Sandra Cisneros, Julia Alvarez, and Lisa Chávez, poetry was in fact the predominant literary form among Latinas throughout the 1960s, '70s, and '80s. Of course, this is not an unknown phenomenon: poetry is almost always the first literary expression of politically driven movements. As Seamus Heaney pointed out in his 1990 Oxford lecture, "The Redress of Poetry": "In any movement toward liberation, it will be necessary to deny the normative authority of the dominant language or literary tradition." For U.S. Latinas, the dominant literary tradition of their formal educations was Anglo-American fiction; the dominant language was and remains English. Thus it is not surprising that poetry employing a great deal of code switching between English and Spanish was the first literary salvo Latina writers fired across the bow of the established order.

Much has been made of a perceived connection between the contemporary written work of U.S. Latino/Latina poets and a "living oral Hispanic literary tradition," as if the only Spanish-language literary exposure available to these writers was via *corridos* (ballads) and hearth-side family *cuentos* (stories). I and others have written extensively elsewhere about the inaccuracy of this perception,[1] but suffice it to say that there did exist throughout the nineteenth and twentieth centuries in the United States a tradition of published Spanish-language literature, including poetry, especially in the popular press. In fact, so prevalent was poetry and short fiction in Spanish-language newspapers of the nineteenth century that it is tempting to claim a far greater level of appreciation for sophisticated literature among Tejanas, Nuevo Mexicanas, and Californianas than among their frontier peers hailing from what would become the "dominant society." Moreover, in the twentieth century, especially during the Mexican Revolution, Spanish-language newspapers throughout the southwestern United States constituted an extremely vibrant literary press (filled with the work of Mexican writers in temporary exile), and in several cases contained extensive feminist social criticism that deeply affected the thinking of the grandmothers of the current generation of Latina writers. It is thus not surprising to find that many contemporary Latinas claim to have much stronger cultural and intellectual ties to their grandparents than to their parents.

Of course, family oral history and storytelling often play a large role in the formation of writers, no matter what their ethnicity or culture. If the prevalence of *abuelita* (grandmother) poems in contemporary Latina literature can be used as a gauge, then it was most often the abuelitas who instructed young Latinas in this country in history (both personal and public) and cultural customs and values. Evangelina Vigil-Piñon's "apprenticeship" is perhaps the quintessential poem of this sort:

> when I join my grandmother
> for a tasa de café
> and I listen to the stories

de su antepasado
her words paint masterpieces
and these I hang
in the galleries of my mind:

I want to be an artist like her. (p. 245)

There is another, sociological reason for this skipping of generational influence. The Great Depression and World War II forced younger women into the workplace, which left their children to be raised at home by the grandmothers.

Thus to argue, as many have, that contemporary Latina writers either evolved out of a purely oral tradition or are simply products of increased access to the American educational system is fallacious. Latina writers who came of age in the 1960s and 1970s evolved out of a rich bicultural and bilingual context in which Spanish-language literary expression was accepted and appreciated *outside* of the mandatory English-only educational system. In essence, the one was honed against the other, resulting in an exceedingly incisive literary tool.

The political awakening of young Mexican Americans during what was termed the Chicano Movement created a sense of cultural nationalism that found its first and most strident voice in poetry. But both the political and literary aspects of the 1960s Chicano Movement were male dominated. Then around 1970, Chicano politicization encountered the American women's liberation movement, at which point many Chicanas' cultural and career restrictions began to dissolve. Liberated, politically experienced, college-educated Chicanas began to explore new directions in bilingual poetry, drama, and fiction, but most especially in poetry. Earlier in the Chicano movement, a stylistic and thematic homogeneity had existed, driven primarily by an almost unconscious need for collective self-definition as *la raza*, as a single people. While a collective sense of Latina sisterhood survives in the literature to this day, individual creative vision has replaced cultural/racial/political unity as the driving force. Likewise, most Latina writers have accepted English as their predominant mode of literary expression, though, as will be discussed below, they have succeeded in reshaping the language to their own ends.

Throughout the 1970s most Chicano small-press publications addressed women's writing in some manner, and new, often short-lived journals devoted exclusively to Latina feminist perspectives began to appear. Yet by the 1980s, mainstream critical acceptance remained elusive, and publication of a Chicana writer by a major American publishing house was still a decade away. As Evangelina Vigil (now Vigil-Piñon) pointed out in her introduction to the 1983 "Woman of Her Word" issue of *Revista Chicano-Riqueña*, "Removed from the mainstream of American literature and barely emerging on the Hispanic literary scene, the creativity of Latina writers exists autonomously."[2] This early use of the term "Latina" over "Chicana" was indicative of another change in the nature of the politicization: Chicanas no longer saw themselves as simply the feminist extension of the Chicano movement, but as an integral part of Third World Feminism. At the same time, Latina writers of non-Mexican heritage began to publish in the United States—women with roots in Puerto Rico, Cuba, the Dominican Republic, and South and Central America—each bringing with them elements of their own national literary traditions. Writing in the second edition (1983) of *This Bridge Called My Back: Writings by Radical Women of Color*, editor Cherríe Moraga acknowledged that "to change the world, we have to change ourselves—even sometimes our most cherished block-hard convictions. As *This Bridge Called My Back* is not written in stone, neither is our political vision. It is subject to change."[3]

The question is often raised why anthologies like this one gather a single group of writers—Latinas, in this case—if the result of the gathering is to emphasize diversity within the group. One answer is simple: for the most part, Latina poetry is simply not available at the average American bookstore. It is only since the 1993 publication of Sandra Cisneros's *Woman Hollering Creek* by Random House that there has been any significant chance at all of finding fiction by U.S. Latina writers in most bookstores and libraries, much less poetry.

Writers like Sandra Cisneros, Oscar Hijuelos, Ana Castillo, Rudolfo Anaya, and Julia Alvarez have recently begun receiving Pulitzers, National Book Awards, MacArthur fellowships, and the like, yet the publishing truism that "awards do not a market make" holds sway here. The mainstream view, though it is evolving, still holds that Latino writers are somewhat "exotic" and thus appeal to a narrowly defined market. That market is made narrower when gender is added to the equation. The nails are firmly in the coffin when these "double minority" writers are writing poetry, the least lucrative of all literary genres. Thus Latina poetry, unless it comes from a writer whose reputation has been previously established by a successful book of fiction, is mainly put in print by university presses and small (often micro) regional independent publishers.

The poets in this anthology truly hail from all over the United States, from New York to North Dakota to Washington to California to Texas to Florida; their families come from Argentina, Brazil, Chile, Cuba, the Dominican Republic, Guatemala, Mexico, Puerto Rico, and Spain, and many have some indigenous "Native American" heritage from, among others, the Maya and Aztec, the Yaqui and Apache, the Chumasch and Lakota. And as in any gathering of Americans, there are also bloodlines that reach into the heart of Europe, Africa, and the Jewish Diaspora. Yet all are labeled Latina or, as the government would have it, Hispanic. Why?

If this anthology's scope relied upon the terminology of the U.S. census form, our endeavor here would be very different. So before venturing into their literary production, we face the question of identity: what constitutes Latina-ness? What binds this group together? Finally, and most important, how does this knowledge of Latina identity issues inform our understanding of the literature of this group of women?

Naming is, of course, an important act in every culture, and we can learn much from the several names that have been applied to this group of women, some of which are more ethnically specific than others, as well as to the names they have chosen for themselves. The term imposed by the U.S. government, Hispanic, is still used by a few writers and critics, but in the main the term is deemed objectionable due to the fact that it correctly refers only to individuals of Spanish heritage. The term is frequently misapplied to refer to all individuals with surnames originating in Spain. In fact, such names were themselves, in general, originally Latin, Arabic (Moorish), or Hebrew cognates. Of course, the question of surnames is moot, since many Latinas have acquired "non-qualifying" names in the normal course of American marriage custom.

"Latina" has become the preferred term among women writers and critics within the last five years, allowing as it does for multiple countries of origin. It refers specifically to women whose ethnic origins lie in Latin America, which the *American Heritage Dictionary* defines as comprising "countries of the Western Hemisphere south of the United States having Spanish or Portuguese as their official languages." The term "Latina" does not refer, as some writers have surmised, to individuals whose linguistic heritage is a Latin-based (Romance) language, since this would include French-speaking Canadians, Italian Americans, etc. "Latina" is a gender-specific term. Both genders are indicated by the admittedly awkward "Latino/a" or "Latina/Latino."

In the interest of greater historical and ethnic specificity, other terms are simultaneously used by Latina/Latino writers and scholars. "Chicano" was used as an inclusive term for Mexican Americans of both genders during the early days of the Chicano *movimiento* (approximately 1965 to 1980). "Chicana" gained currency in the early 1970s when the American women's movement began to affect women active within the Chicano political movement. Both terms still bear considerable political weight. Spelling these terms with an *x* rather than a *ch* (Xicana) emphasizes indigenous Mexican origins. Artist Amalia Mesa-Bains, the first U.S. Latina recipient of a MacArthur "genius award," wrote her 1983 dissertation on culture and identity among Chicana artists. Recently she said: "When I use the word Chicana it has to do with more than ethnic identity. It is a statement about a period of time in my own development, about a moment in history in a collective group. When you use the term Latina, it is a term that can be an umbrella."[4]

Another common term, "Mexican American," is still in use, though some consider it objectionable due to its past implications of second-class citizenship. The term "mestiza" indicates an individual of mixed heritage. This term was one of sixteen developed by the Spanish in Mexico and used throughout Latin America to designate various mixtures of indigenous, black, and Spanish blood, each with its own placement in Spain's colonial hierarchical class structure. Partially in rebellion against the Spanish overlords, "mestiza" was widely adopted and came to mean anyone of mixed heritage who was not of the ruling class. Also derived from the colonial period is the term "Hispana," which indicates women of "pure" Spanish extraction. This term retained currency in California and New Mexico, where racial and class distinctions were maintained well into the nineteenth century, and in some rural locales, well into the twentieth century.

Other terms, such as "Cubana," "Puertorriqueña," "Tejana," "Californiana," and "Mexicana" indicate Latinas with roots or residency in various geographic regions. "Nuyorican," perhaps the latest addition to this body of terminology, refers to New Yorkers of Puerto Rican heritage.

One of the Latina writers who has taken a scholarly interest in the matter of identity is poet and novelist Ana Castillo. Defining herself as "mestiza/Mexic Amerindian," Castillo writes in *Massacre of the Dreamers: Essays on Xicanisma* that the group labeled as

Latina or Hispanic in the United States can be neither "summarized nor neatly categorized." Even so, in terms of literature, Castillo points out that "throughout the history of the United States 'I' as subject and object has been reserved for white authorship and readership" and that Latinas, regardless of their diversity, have suffered the considerable and inevitable educational, economic, and psychological consequences of that fact."[5] In a sense, she is defining identity by exclusion: I am she who does *not* appear, Castillo seems to say, in canonical American literature, in American media, on the cover of American fashion magazines.

"An identity problem is obvious," writes Beverly Sánchez-Padilla in her poem about the figurative mother of all mestizas, Malintzín, the translator/adviser/lover of the conquistador Hernán Cortés (p. 203). Malintzín came to be known by the Spanish name Doña Marina, as well as by the derogatory appellations La Malinche (the traitor) and La Chingada (the violated, or worse, the whore). Carmen Tafolla, in her poem on this topic, "La Malinche," sees Malintzín as being very aware of her role in history. Tafolla has Malintzín cry out:

> But Chingada I was not.
>> Not tricked, not screwed, not traitor.
> For I was not traitor to myself—
>> I saw a dream
>> and I reached it.
>>> *Another world . . .*
>>>> La raza.
>>>> La raaaaaaaa-zaaaaa . . .
>>>>> (p. 219)

Malintzín's predicament is a common subject in Latina writing, even among authors of non-Mexican origin. Castigated as a whore and a traitor by many writers over the years, Malintzín is for Tafolla a visionary realist who defeats the Spanish invasion in the only way possible, by giving birth to a new mestiza race that will survive the conquest and thus inherit its own ancestral lands. As indigenous peoples have always named themselves throughout the Americas, in Tafolla's poem Malintzín calls this new race "the people"—*la raza*.

This central figure in the history of the Americas is also the subject of poems by Victoria García-Galaviz (p. 132) and by Angela de Hoyos. In fact, one of De Hoyos's most important poems is "La Malinche a Cortés y Vice Versa" (p. 112), which is cast in the form of a dramatic dialogue. Malintzín (here Marina) is described by De Hoyos as a bright survivor, a sensitive and intelligent woman speaking boldly to her conqueror. Marina suggests to Cortés that they carve their names in the sand, an image that plays the temporary against the timeless, the ever-changing seashore versus the eternal sands of time. But Cortés, a male chauvinist pig if ever there was one, rejects the idea out of hand. The whole world, he says, knows you are "mi querida Marina. No necesitas/adornos superfluos." Love is enough, he concludes. The implication is that Cortés could not bear the idea of actually *marrying* a barefoot Indian, no matter how great her charms might be: "Es cierto,/es una hembra/a todo dar . . ." (It's true, as a woman she's a real knockout . . .). Marina's anger rises as she names Cortés a "gringo desabrido" (insensitive foreigner). De Hoyos created in this 1979 poem a profound and enduring metaphor for both the feminist/machismo dichotomy in contemporary Latina/Latino culture and the Latino/Norteño cultural collision.

Malinche's character and her role as an intercultural bridge are alluded to both directly and obliquely throughout Latina literature. Documenting a contemporary and very different sort of cultural collision, Lorna Dee Cervantes describes life as a young streetwise pachuca in her poem "Bird Ave" (p. 66). Conjuring up the 1960s with lines lifted from rock and roll songs of that era, Cervantes's characters "Cat-eyes, me and Mousie" rule their corner of their barrio (neighborhood) with rhythm, hip grace, and a cold-eyed clarity:

> we knew it all
> the code and the symbology
> the poetics and the order
> of place and gesture
> we were honed for the killing
> primed for the time
> . . . .
> *Don't Fuck with Us*
> our motto
> *We're Here to Serve*
> the ruse
> *Listen Watch*
> *Be Silent*
> was the Conquest's
> hidden code

Like Malinche / Malintzín, alluded to in the last four lines quoted, these girls proclaim that they are not las chingadas, they are the initiators, they hold the power: "we were better/than military/ beauty brains & brass/man/we were the trinity." Yet for all their assertions of power through group identification, they remain vulnerable: "man/it was tough/to know it all/and we haven't/ learned anything/since."

Chicanas have traced their roots even beyond historical figures like Malintzín, Our Lady of Guadalupe, and Sor Juana Inés de la Cruz into a purely American mythos, developing the Aztec pantheon into a source of literary symbolism and allusion, similar to the way European poets of a prior age mined Greco-Roman mythology. Sheila Sánchez-Hatch successfully fuses contemporary and mythological imagery in her poem "Coatlícue" (p. 143), which is openly about identity:

Days after atomic bomb days drop
and so I seek knowledge of the modern unknown
through the ancient ways.
Counsel me, Coatlícue,
she of the serpent skirt
. . . .
Oh, Universal Duality
where do we fit into your Aztec cosmology?

The poem's narrator strives to define something beyond geography, history, or even racial origin that empowers contemporary Latina identity—a recognizable culture held in common, even though individual manifestations of that culture in literature may be ascribed to one or another ethnic or national origin.

This commonality is evident in reader response as well. The absolute joy in a young Latina's face that accompanies the shock of self-recognition when she first encounters a work like Sandra Cisneros's *House on Mango Street* is a delicious, if all too rare, experience in the life of a teacher. The fact that the book is set in Chicago, and that the *cultura* described is specifically Mexican American *del norte*, seems to matter not at all to young Latina readers, whether they are Puertorriqueñas living in New York or Cubanas in Miami or seventh-generation Californianas in East L.A. The fact of the matter is that for this group which cannot be "summarized or categorized," the I of the texts from which they learned to read, the I of the books they studied in school, was seldom if ever an I with which Latinas could identify; certainly, it was never truly *yo*. Esperanza of Mango Street seems to function as Everywoman for young Latina readers, even if the chilly urban street culture of Chicano Chicago is far removed from the culture of agrarian migrants of the Midwest or the Southwest, or the unique insular cultures of Caribbean immigrants, or that of the political visionaries of Aztlán.

At the root of this common culture is the fact that Spanish, often the first language of U.S. Latinas or of their parents, constitutes a deeply cherished transnational/transhistorical linguistic umbilical cord. Except in the case of older writers and a few first-generation émigrés, Spanish is seldom the dominant language of either daily use or literary expression. Still, throughout the literature created by U.S.-based Latina writers, there is an undercurrent of love for the Spanish language, whether or not the writer herself is fluent. This is evident in the code switching that occurs, especially in poetry, when a Spanish word or phrase is used within an English context when the Spanish is more accurate or more evocative than its English equivalent. This bilingualism, denigrated by terms like "Spanglish" and "Tex-Mex," is actually one of the most powerful linguistic tools at the disposal of these writers. Masters of this technique, such as Angela de Hoyos, Carmen Tafolla, or Evangelina Vigil-Piñon, have created distinct poetic idioms, at once reflective of the bilingual culture they inhabit and rising above it as a sort of linguistic critique, ennobling and empowering the language with nuance and beauty. Other writers, such as Lucha Corpi, have chosen to write poetry in Spanish and fiction in English. Included in *¡Floricanto Sí!* are also writers such as Puertorriqueñas Giannina Braschi and Rosario Ferré, who write exclusively in Spanish. Corpi and Braschi have developed long-term trusting relationships with their translators, respectively Catherine Rodríguez-Nieto and Tess O'Dwyer; Ferré prefers to translate her own work.

But this "linguistic umbilical cord" is evident in more than simply the usage of the Spanish language. Lillian Castillo-Speed, in her introduction to *Latina: Women's Voices from the Borderlands*, writes that Latina literature appears to English-language readers "to have been newly translated from Spanish, when in fact new Latina writers have taken the English language and have made it their own. It is more than just a combination of English and Spanish: it reflects the reality of women who live in two worlds."[6]

In the case of Mexican American women, Chicanas, a very

real border divides their reality in half, often separating *la familia* into branches inhabiting two vastly different linguistic, economic, cultural, educational, and social worlds. But aside from geographic divisions, there is a substantial gender-based division as well. Latin American machismo continues to this day to forge a special bond among women family members, a bond that surfaces in the literature as both a consistent theme and a predominant subject. This is reinforced by powerful mother figures. As one writer put it, "No Latina can say to another, 'la cocina de mi mamá,' and be misunderstood. It is always the same kitchen, with the same rules and rituals." Lorna Dee Cervantes, in her poem "Beneath the Shadow of the Freeway," describes *la familia*, and the two worlds she inhabits, this way:

> We were a woman family:
> Grandma, our innocent Queen;
> Mama, the Swift Knight, Fearless Warrior.
> . . . .
> Myself: I could never decide.
> So I turned to books, those staunch, upright men.
> I became Scribe: Translator of Foreign Mail,
> interpreting letters from the government, notices
> of dissolved marriages and Welfare stipulations. (p. 62)

Finally there is the female bonding created by the historical influence of the male-dominated Catholic Church, which provides Latina writers with a rich source of imagery, a target for rebellion (and an almost inexhaustible well of guilt), as well as a set of established personally relevant rituals such as *quinceañeras* (the traditional presentation of fifteen-year-old girls to society as marriageable young women). Family holds the sort of primacy in Latina literature that it did for, say, Jane Austen—the world revolves around the family. Thus the disturbance of *la familia* by international boundary lines, by evolving sociopolitical viewpoints, by lapses in generational communication due to the development of English as a predominant language, and by temporal distance from their root cultures are all powerful factors in the lives of these writers, forcing them to live in "two worlds."

To be a Latina living in the United States is to be separated in some way from a remembered root culture, however idealized it might be, whether the divisive element is a line on a map, an ocean, or time itself. To inhabit such a reality requires balance. Gloria Anzaldúa, in her brilliant 1987 essay "The New Mestiza," describes the development of a bilingual, bicultural, transgenerational balancing act and suggests that the "new" mestiza's identity has more to do with bicultural adaptation than it does with blended ethnicities:

> The new *mestiza* copes by developing a tolerance for contradictions, a tolerance for ambiguity. She learns to be an Indian in Mexican culture, to be Mexican from an Anglo point of view. She learns to juggle cultures. She has a plural personality, she operates in a pluralistic mode—nothing is thrust out, the good the bad and the ugly, nothing rejected, nothing abandoned. Not only does she sustain contradictions, she turns the ambivalence into something else.
>
> She can be jarred out of ambivalence by an intense, and often painful, emotional event which inverts or resolves the ambivalence. . . . It is work that the soul performs. That focal point or fulcrum, that juncture where the *mestiza* stands, is where phenomena tend to collide. It is where the possibility of uniting all that is separate occurs. This assembly is not one where severed or separated pieces merely come together. Nor is it a balancing act of opposing powers. In attempting to work out a synthesis, the self has added a third element which is greater than the sum of its severed parts. That third element is a new consciousness—a *mestiza* consciousness—and though it is a source of intense pain, its energy comes from continual creative motion.[7]

Yet Pat Mora, a Chicana poet from El Paso who has certainly mastered the synthesis described by Anzaldúa in her professional life, writes of the situation of being caught between worlds in terms that can only be seen as "opposing powers." Repeatedly the poet describes crossing, as a successful Chicana in a superficial and vaguely dangerous Anglo world, back into a world that is safer, more real somehow. In her poem "Sonrisas," Mora writes of living "in a doorway/between two rooms"—a boardroom inhabited by "careful women in crisp beige/suits, quick beige smiles" and "the other room" where "señoras/in faded dresses stir sweet/milk coffee, laughter whirls" (p. 165). In "Bilingual Christmas" Mora juxtaposes the images of an eggnog-and-rum-balls office party with the poverty outside the windows where "we hear/whimpering/children too cold/to sing/on Christmas Eve." (p. 166). This sort of poetic documentation of living between two very different worlds and functioning in both is a theme that occurs again and again throughout all U.S. Latina literature. It is worth noting that this theme is conspicuously absent in most Latin American women's writing.

Throughout the Chicano movement and into the 1980s, both male and female poets incorporated more or less overtly political messages relevant to the Chicano situation in the United States. The poems of Cervantes, De Hoyos, Tafolla, and Mora, mentioned above, are good examples of this, as is Ana Castillo's well-known poem "In My Country" (p. 53), which describes a virtual utopia by listing all the American realities that her "country" does not share. The 1980s shift to identification with Third World Feminism helped refocus the political content of Latina poetry. Much of Marjorie Agosín's poetry, for example, deals with human rights abuses throughout South America. Pina Pipino's "White Scarves" (p. 185) deals with the women of the Plaza de Mayo in Buenos Aires. Beatriz Rivera's "Lament of the Terrorist" (p. 192) describes the mental anguish of a guerrilla in suicide-attack mode. Such examples are numerous.

The most famous political poem contained in ¡Floricanto Sí! is without doubt Demetria Martínez's "Nativity: For Two Salvadoran Women, 1986–1987" (p. 162). Martínez was indicted in December 1987 on charges of aiding and abetting the entry of two Salvadoran women into the United States, making her the first (and only) journalist to be prosecuted in connection with sanctuary work. "Nativity" was used in evidence against Martínez—one of the very few times in U.S. history when a poem has been so used against its author. Martínez was acquitted of all charges.

Besides themes of identity, mythology, family, bicultural/binational realities, and politics/human rights, readers of ¡Floricanto Sí! will notice several cultural/historical icons recurring both as symbols and subjects, with Our Lady of Guadalupe (la Virgen) and artist Frida Kahlo at opposing poles, and curanderas (mystical folk healers) and field hands in between. Then there is love and sexuality. While this volume contains some love poems, both hetero and same-sex in orientation, Latina poetry is often so wrapped in sensual metaphors that actual love poems can be almost indistinguishable from poems about desert landscapes or food or death! Even though such an assertion verges on being a cliché, it is a fact that a deep sensuality empowers almost all Latina imagery, whether the topic is a saint's dying moment—"once again she would dip the iron bar into the coals,/and pass it gently like a magician's wand over her skin—/to feel the passion that flames for a moment,/in all dying things" (p. 90), a slant of light—"Dusk catches in the crook of her elbow,/in the sleeve she raises to wipe her face" (p. 60), or a sexual encounter—"you touch me with those potter's hands/that for centuries have fondled clay/into song./I taste you in the heat of mezcal,/in the sweetness of orange slices" (p. 229). Such intensely sensual imagery gives Latina poetry much of its appeal as well as much of its power, especially when topics themselves are of intellectual or existential consequence: "I am no Circe," writes Deborah Parédez, "no magical powers/no victim of narrative/just a woman with these few words/a woman who has peered through the barrel of a loaded gun/leaving nothing intact" (p. 178).

The poems contained in this volume were selected in stages. First, certain poems were chosen for their historical and/or aesthetic value, whether the authors are now familiar names or not. Next, Latina poets who have published books or chapbooks, or who have had substantial appearances in literary magazines, were invited by letter to submit. Finally, an open call for submissions was advertised. We were delighted in the end to meet many poets of whom we were unaware, often living in areas not traditionally associated with Latino/Latina communities. In the main, the criteria for inclusion were aesthetic quality and cultural depth.

We have included the dates of composition for each poem, thus allowing the reader to place the poems within a historical context. Appended at the back of this volume is a glossary of Spanish language terms and phrases that occur in predominantly English poems. Poems written entirely in Spanish are here printed in their original form, accompanied by translations either by the author herself or by a translator selected by the author.

Languages other than English that occur within an English text are traditionally set in italics. This practice, however, while still followed by some Latina writers, has itself acquired political overtones. Some writers now maintain that because the bilingual idiom is so much a part of Latina cultural expression, Spanish and English should not be so overtly distinguished in their texts. We have respected the individual preferences of the authors in this matter.

There is a Penguin anthology on just about every topic of interest to some group of readers somewhere on the planet. It says a lot that this is the first Penguin anthology devoted to Latina writers in the United States. *¡Floricanto Sí!* celebrates the work of Latina poets because as a group they are producing a remarkable body of work that interprets America to itself in genuinely new ways, employing new terms and new perspectives. *¡Floricanto Sí!*

celebrates the individual, diverse voices of this group because within this amazing multiplicity we find a new poetic sensibility emerging from a still-evolving mestiza consciousness. We are watching an ancient nebula birth new stars.

Bryce Milligan
San Antonio, Tejas
1997

NOTES

1. See the introduction to *Daughters of the Fifth Sun: A Collection of Latina Fiction and Poetry* (New York: Putnam/Riverhead, 1995), edited by Milligan, Milligan, and De Hoyos. See also "Ever Radical: A Survey of Tejana Writers" by Bryce Milligan, in *Texas Women Writers* (College Station: Texas A&M University Press, 1997), pp. 207–46, edited by Sylvia Grider and Lou Rodenberger.
2. Evangelina Vigil, ed., "Woman of Her Word: Hispanic Women Write," special issue of *Revista Chicano-Riqueña* XI, 3–4 (1983), p. 7.
3. Cherríe Moraga, "Introduction," in *This Bridge Called My Back: Writings by Radical Women of Color*, edited by Cherríe Moraga and Gloria Anzaldúa, 2nd edition (Latham, NY: Kitchen Table/Women of Color Press, 1983), p. (iii).
4. Noni Mendoza Reis and Irene McGinty, eds., *Women of Hope: Latinas Abriendo Camino Study Guide* (New York: Bread and Roses Cultural Project, 1995), p. 43.
5. Ana Castillo, *Massacre of the Dreamers: Essays on Xicanisma* (Albuquerque: University of New Mexico Press, 1994), pp. 1–8.
6. Lillian Castillo-Speed, ed., *Latina: Women's Voices from the Borderlands* (New York: Simon & Schuster, 1995), pp. 17–18.
7. Gloria Anzaldúa, *Borderlands/La Frontera: The New Mestiza* (San Francisco: Spinsters/Aunt Lute Books, 1987), pp. 79–80.

¡FLORICANTO SÍ!

❧ ❧ ❧

🐌 TERESA PALOMO ACOSTA

The corn tortilla
1994

The creation of the divine,
the corn tortilla,
has nothing to do
with a man finding himself
a tortillera to marry. A woman who
will agree to fill in the space between
tortilla feedings with
her body laid out upon the floor mat
for him to step over.
Yes, let's be honest here.

The creation of the divine,
the corn tortilla,
has instead
so much to do
with picking
the right hour,
comal, mixing bowl.
The masa de harina itself.
Which is waiting on the shelves of anyplace
she calls home at the moment.

The creation of the divine,
the corn tortilla,
requires
that she and her comadres have time to exchange tips, leisurely,
over café, on street corners:

Un poco de esto, un poquito de aquello.
The creation of the divine,
the corn tortilla,
has nothing to do with a fake recipe:
Yes, let's be honest here again.

I mean we have no corn tortilla recetas
despite Diana Kennedy's expensive cookbook
admonitions. Nor do we subscribe to
the "great" American cuisine newsletter tips.
And we put no faith in pricey cups
measuring the necessary water
nor in thermometers taking the exactly precise temperature
of the comal.

The creation of the divine,
the corn tortilla,
has much, however, to do with
the joy with which to overcome
the melancholy that overwhelms you in
a supermercado where Mejicano merchandisers have
reduced the corn tortilla to flavorless paper that evaporates
seconds after you slap it on the tongue.
Yes, the supermercado
where Mejicano merchandisers have sold out
the righteous tortillera,
and her calling to set out
fat and solid corn tortillas
in front of people
in the center of the table,
wrapped in a little trapito.

The creation,
utterly and completely,

of the divine,
the corn tortilla,
comes with a simple set of instructions to wise Mejicanas
cocinando anywhere that we live:
just enough masa,
just enough heat,
just enough time.
Nothing more. nothing less.
Commit this to memory, mija.

This set of non-instructions is
brought to you from the oral tradition cookbook (authors—las
mujeres; circa—you name it)

On the back cover
a corn tortilla story: peeks out of a trapito.
Everybody sits in a circle
and passes that trapito
'round and 'round.
Round and Round.
Like the real lone star of texas should have been.

In the season of change
1994

If E. Dickinson and I had been friends,
we would have each owned a treasure chest
filled with doilies for laying under our silverware,
for showing off atop our china cabinets.
For softening the scars in the 300-year-old dining room tables
we would have inherited
from our great-grandmothers.

But our bisabuelas never met,
exchanged glances or
sat next to each other in church.
And I only discovered E. Dickinson
in the few pages she was allowed
to enter in my high school literature texts.

Only years later did
I finally pore over her words,
believing that
her songs held
my name inscribed within.
And that they might fill the air
with the ancient signs of kinship
that women can choose to pass along.

And thus left on our own,
E. Dickinson and I
sat down at the same table,
savoring her rhubarb pie and my cafecito,
chatting and chismeando
and trading secrets
despite decrees demanding silence between us:

women from separate corners of the room.

Today the pomegranate tree was in bloom
1995

Today, despite the fact
that we didn't even glance its way
and wasted our lunch hour
at the mall, chasing down
nonfat gourmet tortilla chips
put out by a mega corporation,
the branches of la pomegranate
were enlaced with petal upon petal.

Today, despite the fact
that our eyes refused to move off
our account ledgers and
the taxes we were adding up
or the mortgages we were refinancing at the bank,
la pomegranate leaned itself against the streetlight pole
and spilled June in my face.

It brushed against my left eyelid
as I ambled aimlessly next to it.
It startled me into forgetting
that notes and messages were waiting
for me at home.

It spread
its thick love over me,
releasing a dangerous invitation
to sit in the shade of the porch,
remembering el tío's long-ago raspas
the color of pomegranates.

It is an exquisite fading away, I think
1996

The book reports that along Highway One,
between Vietnam and Cambodia,
a once "exquisitely" painted ceiling of
Vietnam masters with their subjects and servants
is fading away. Lost to time and war. The weather,
probably. And new painters contemplating it, I hope,
with new paintbrushes and new paint.

How glad I am to know the painting has chipped
and seems to be passing into nothing
but a wall, blank again, waiting
for other artists to dabble
—perhaps with white for lilies
or bluegreen for waves from the beach along
the road called Highway One
between Vietnam y Cambodia.

I'm almost certain
that this fading away picture was painted
in strokes to soften the lines between:
the master and his wife,
their requisite children,
the many subjects,
the many more servants.
The truth about having
more than you need.
About having almost nothing.

I'm almost certain that the painter blurred them together,
leaning one into the other to make us think
that this was the real story: Soft. Gentle.

No shouting in the face.
No lashes of the whip evident on the neck.

But, when I think of my own historia
as a mejicana en tejas/aztlán, norte amerika,
I know they all led separate lives.

And so I believe that
it is an exquisite fading away
of at least this painting.
I bet that there are so many more,
perhaps even in living color
along this same Highway One.
And in neighboring Burma.
And in museums depicting colonial Inglaterra or
el westward moving the U S of A.
And also in sold and bought Mexico and Africa.
Y en algunas otras de mis tierras: España,
Tejas
And of course en las Carolinas:
There are more retratos of jefes surrounded
by their minions.

Well,
I've had my fill
of such paintings.

I want Highway One
to sing instead
with whitewashed walls
so we, the people, can loosen our tongues,
tell our cuentos and
regain our dignity.
Learn to laugh again—for ourselves.

Forgetting forever
the grinning court jester's smiles
we surely had on our faces
in those "exquisite" paintings of
jefe/sujeto/servidor.

❧ MARJORIE AGOSÍN

Marta Alvarado, profesora de historia
1994

I
En setiembre,
más allá de las
brisas, del humo,
cuando el otoño deshoja su
caparazón de fuego,
pienso en ti,
frágil y severa,
pequeña y agigantada.

II
Viajera por demenciales y sutiles geografías
con tu vara encantada, cantarina,
nos contabas sobre Yugoslavia
y el Líbano
Chile y Perú.
Esos detalles de las láminas imaginarias, dudosas
te perdías
y diciendo que la verdadera
historia la hacían las mujeres,
las mujeres-niñas
y las ancianas mujeres.

III
Cuando los niños de la guerra
son una llama nebulosa,
cuando la caparazón de la tierra

es un chal incendiado de oros,
Te nombro, Marta Alvarado,
llegando casi de madrugada
con tus huesudos guantes de lana,
para abrir la puerta de la escuela
y la llama del cuaderno.

Marta Alvarado, History Professor
1994

I
In September
beyond the
breezes and the smoke
when autumn unveils its
fiery shell,
I think of you
fragile and severe,
small and immense

II
You were a
traveler through demented and subtle geographies
with your magic wand singing
about Yugoslavia
and Lebanon
Chile and Peru
—Those details on imaginary sheets, doubtful
you would get lost
because true
history was made by women
the girl-women
and the old women.

III
When the children of war
become a nebulous flame,
when the earth's shell
is a shawl afire with gold,
I name you, Marta Alvarado,

arriving almost at dawn
with your bony woolen gloves
to open the school's doors
and the defiance of your notebook.

English translation by the author

Umiliana Cárdenas, pescadora de poetas
1995

Salida
del tiempo
de las sirenas
y los pescados ceremoniosos,
toda humedecida y cantarina,
con sus años cargados
de escamas
de inverosímiles
fragancias y de
piedras transitorias,
sale del mar
precaria y gigante,
Umiliana Cárdenas.
Ofrece poemas
a cincuenta pesos cada uno
y cincuenta recetas para
cocer papas.
Es de las islas más islas que el cielo,
donde el viento presagia
nacimientos y muertes,
donde la vida es una esquina dorada
de azares y tiempos mudos.

Umiliana Cárdenas,
Fisher-Poet
1995

Since
the time
of the sirens
and the ceremonial fishermen,
wet and full of song,
her years filled
with scales
of unbelievable
fragrances and the
transient stones,
she has emerged from the sea
Umiliana Cárdenas,
precarious and oversized.
She offers us poems
at fifty pesos each,
and fifty recipes
for cooking potatoes.
She is from the islands more insular than the sky,
where the wind foresees
births and deaths,
where life is a golden corner
of orange blossoms and unspoken times.

English translation by the author

El credo de Titania
1996

I

Gobernaría
con un consejo
de hadas violetas,
con olor a lilas y patchoulí,
danzarinas en
la fragilidad,
de la paz
del tul.

II

Me guiaría por
la fragancia, como una
presencia.

III

Para conversar con
los muertos,
oiría el acertado tono,
les pediría a ellas, las hadas,
los dones necesarios
para el gobierno propicio:
un trocito de alegría
incondicional
otras ramas de cordura.

IV

Seguiría consejos tales
como la necesidad
de aprender a nombrar

las estrellas,
los árboles extinguidos,
todo lo ambiguo y gentil
y el caminar tras la espesura
de las noches malvas.

V

Gobernaría
desde un globo de aire,
no tendría palacios ni oficinas oscuras,
sólo el cielo.
Dicen que hay mucha paz y silencio
en las alturas.
Instalaría a mi consejo de hadas
tras un sauce,
tras un cristal.
Serviría el agua de los ríos verdes
como el vino más cálido a las gargantas tibias.

VI

Me rodearía de las hadas, de todas las presencias
que son alientos,
semillas doradas
en la oscuridad.

VII

No habrían fronteras,
tan solo los ojos
de los justos.

VIII

Me vestiría de blanco,
repartiría almendras

y palomas,
volantines de
chocolate
sin fronteras,
en un sueño de umbrales.

Titania's Creed
1996

I
I would rule
with a council
of violet fairies,
with the smell of lilacs and patchouli
dancers of
fragility,
of the peace
of tulle.

II
I would guide myself
by scent, like a
presence.

III
I would converse with
the dead,
I would ask them, the fairies,
for the gifts necessary
for proper government
a little piece of unconditional
happiness
other branches of sanity.

IV
I would follow their advice:
the necessity

of learning to name
the stars,
the extinct trees,
all that is ambiguous and gentle
and the walk across the thickness
of mauve nights.

V

I would rule
from a hot air balloon,
I would not have palaces or dark offices,
only the sky.
They say there is much peace and silence
in heights.
I would install my council of fairies
behind a willow,
behind a crystal.
I would serve water from the green rivers
like the warmest wine
to warm throats.

VI

I would surround myself with the fairies, each presence
a breath,
a golden seed
in the darkness.

VII

There would be no borders,
only the eyes
of the just.

VIII
I would wear white,
I would hand out almonds
and pigeons,
chocolates
in a dream of thresholds.

English translation by the author

❧ JULIA ALVAREZ

Homecoming
1994

When my cousin Carmen married, the guards
at her father's *finca* took the guests' bracelets
and wedding rings and put them in an armored truck
for safekeeping while wealthy, dark-skinned men,
their plump, white women and spoiled children
bathed in a river whose bottom had been cleaned
for the occasion. She was Tío's only daughter;
and he wanted to show her husband's family,
a bewildered group of sunburnt Minnesotans,
that she was valued. He sat me at their table
to show off my English, and when he danced with me,
fondling my shoulder blades beneath my bridesmaid's gown
as if they were breasts, he found me skinny
but pretty at seventeen, and clever.
Come back from that cold place, Vermont, he said,
all this is yours! Over his shoulder
a dozen workmen hauled in blocks of ice
to keep the champagne lukewarm and stole
glances at the wedding cake, a dollhouse duplicate
of the family rancho, the shutters marzipan,
the cobbles almonds. A maiden aunt housekept,
touching up whipped cream roses with a syringe
of eggwhites, rescuing the groom when the heat
melted his chocolate shoes into the frosting.
On too much rum Tío led me across the dance floor,
dusted with talcum for easy gliding, a smell

of babies underfoot. He twirled me often,
excited by my pleas of dizziness, teasing me
that my merengue had lost its Caribbean.
Above us, Chinese lanterns strung between posts
came on and one snapped off and rose
into a purple postcard sky.
A grandmother cried: *The children all grow up too fast.*
The Minnesotans finally broke loose and danced a Charleston
and were pronounced good gringos with latino hearts.
The little sister, freckled with a week of beach,
her hair as blonde as movie stars', was asked
by maids if they could touch her hair or skin,
and she backed off, until it was explained to her,
they meant no harm. *This is all yours,*
Tío whispered, pressing himself into my dress.
The workmen costumed in their workclothes danced
a workman's jig. The maids went by with trays
of wedding bells and matchbooks monogrammed
with Dick's and Carmen's names. It would be years
before I took the courses that would change my mind
in schools paid for by sugar from the fields around us,
years before I could begin to comprehend
how one does not see the maids when they pass by
with trays of deviled eggs arranged in daisy wheels.
—It was too late, or early, to be wise—
The sun was coming up beyond the amber waves
of cane, the roosters crowed, the band struck up
Las Mañanitas, a morning serenade. I had a vision
that I blamed on the champagne:
the fields around us were burning. At last
a yawning bride and groom got up and cut
the wedding cake, but everyone was full
of drink and eggs, roast pig, and rice and beans.

Except the maids and workmen,
sitting on stoops behind the sugar house,
ate with their fingers from their open palms
windows, shutters, walls, pillars, doors,
made from the cane they had cut in the fields.

The Dashboard Virgencita
1980

🐌 *In César Chávez country, one of my young white students wrote an essay in which she criticized how local Mexican people put the Virgin Mary on their dashboard. "It's in poor taste," she argued, "not to mention kind of sacrilegious."*

La Virgen on the dashboard is good taste
if you speak Spanish and believe in God.
Never mind the bumper stickers
or the nodding dog that agrees with everyone,
the showy vans on display on the highway
with seventy-miles-an-hour Salvador Dalís.
That's them, the white folks, who grew up in English
and believe driving is a practicing religion.
They've made their cars into false gods
and think the radio's revelation.
We know Who to thank when we get there.
We know just a couple of years ago
we would have required angels to move this fast.
With the help of our dashboard Virgencita
we'll keep up with them, pass them.
Maybe She'll raise one of her hands
and wave, jangle her dangling rosary
at them like a broken chain
She'll think of something to teach them a lesson.
And we, we'll have good taste once we've eaten
the fruit of our cheap pickings in their Edens.

Dusting

1984

Each morning I wrote my name
on the dusty cabinet, then crossed
the dining table in script, scrawled
in capitals on the backs of chairs,
practicing signatures like scales
while Mother followed, squirting
linseed from a burping can
into a crumpled-up flannel.

She erased my fingerprints
from the bookshelf and rocker;
polished mirrors on the desk
scribbled with my alphabets.
My name was swallowed in the towel
with which she jeweled the table tops.
The grain surfaced in the oak
and the pine grew luminous.
But I refused with every mark
to be like her, anonymous.

Audition
1995

Porfirio drove Mami and me
to Cook's mountain village
to find a new pantry maid.
Cook had given Mami a tip
that her hometown was girl-heavy,
the men lured away to the cities.
We drove to the interior,
climbing a steep, serpentine,
say-your-last-prayers road.
I leaned toward my mother
as if my weight could throw
the car's balance away
from the sheer drop below.
Late morning we entered
a dusty village of huts.
Mami rolled down her window
and queried an old woman,
Did she know of any girls
looking for work as maids?
Soon we were surrounded
by a dozen señoritas.
Under the thatched cantina
Mami conducted interviews—
a mix of personal questions
and Sphinx-like intelligence tests.
Do you have children, a novio?
Would you hit a child who hit you?
If I give you a quarter to buy
guineos at two for a nickel,
how many will you bring back?

As she interviewed I sat by,
looking the girls over;
one of them would soon
be telling me what to do,
reporting my misbehaviors.
Most seemed nice enough,
befriending me with smiles,
exclamations on my good hair,
my being such a darling.
Those were the ones I favored.
I'd fool them with sweet looks,
improve my bad reputation.
As we interviewed we heard
by the creek that flowed nearby
a high, clear voice singing
a plaintive lullaby . . .
as if the sunlight filling
the cups of the allamandas,
the turquoise sky dappled
with angelfeather clouds,
the creek trickling down
the emerald green of the mountain
had found a voice in her voice.
We listened. Mami's hard-line,
employer-to-be face
softened with quiet sweetness.
The voice came closer, louder—
a slender girl with a basket
of wrung rags on her head
passed by the cantina,
oblivious to our presence.
Who is she? my mother asked.
Gladys, the girls replied.

Gladys! my mother called
as she would for months to come.
Gladys, come clear the plates!
Gladys, answer the door!
Gladys! The young girl turned—
Abruptly, her singing stopped.

GLORIA ANZALDÚA

Cihuatlyotl, *Woman Alone*
1986

Many years   I have fought off your hands, *Raza*
father mother church your rage at my desire to be
with myself, alone.   I have learned to
erect barricades   arch my back against you
thrust   back fingers, sticks   to shriek   no to
kick and claw   my way out of your heart   And
as I grew   you hacked away at the pieces   of
me   that were different   attached your tentacles
to my face and breasts put a lock between my legs.
I had to do it,   *Raza,*   turn my back on your
crookening finger beckoning   beckoning   your
soft brown landscape, tender *nopalitos*.   Oh,   it
was hard,   *Raza*   to cleave flesh from flesh I
risked us both   bleeding to death.   It took   a
long time   but   I learned   to
let your values   roll off   my body   like water
those I swallow I stay alive   become tumors in
my belly.   I refuse   to be taken   over   by things
people   who fear that hollow aloneness
beckoning   beckoning.   No self, only race *vecin-*
dad familia.   My soul has always been yours
one spark   in the roar of your fire.   We Mexicans
are   collective animals.   This I accept   but my
life's work   requires autonomy   like oxygen.
This lifelong battle has ended, *Raza*.   I don't
need to flail against   you. *Raza india mexicana*
norteamericana,   there's no more you can chop off

or graft on me that will change my soul.   I remain who I am, multiple and one of the herd, yet not of it.   I walk on the ground of my own being browned and hardened by the ages.   I am fully formed   carved   by the hands of the ancients, drenched with   the stench of today's headlines. But my own hands whittle   the final work   me

The Cannibal's Canción
1976

It is our custom
   to consume
   the person we love.
   Taboo flesh: swollen
   genitalia   nipples
   the scrotum   the vulva
   the soles of the feet
   the palms of the hand
   heart and liver taste best.
   Cannibalism is blessed.

I'll wear your jawbone
round my neck
listen to your vertebrae
bone tapping bone in my wrists.
I'll string your fingers round my waist—
what a rigorous embrace.
Over my heart I'll wear
a brooch with a lock of your hair.
Nights   I'll sleep cradling
your skull   sharpening
my teeth on your toothless grin.

Sundays there's Mass and communion
and I'll put your relics to rest.

La curandera
1986

I'll tell you how I became a healer.
I was sick, my leg had turned white.
Sobrino went to Juan Dávila
asked if Juan Dávila knew
anyone who could cure me.
Yes, Juan Dávila told him,
there is a healer in Mexico.

Juan Dávila crossed the border
to bring the healer.
When Juan Dávila didn't come back,
Sobrino followed him and found the healer dead.
Sobrino's leg became white
Juan Dávila prayed and prayed
Sobrino died.
Juan Dávila thought,
"It doesn't matter if one is sick or not
what matters is that one thinks so."
In his mind Sobrino wanted to die
In his mind he thought he was dying
so he died.

The Border Patrol came
found *el sobrino* dead.
We'll take the body back to the other side, they said.
No, said Juan Dávila, I'll bury him here.
Under the ground it doesn't matter
which side of the border you're in.
When they were out of sight
Juan Dávila opened his eyes.

Juan Dávila went back across the border
The Border Patrol said no way.
She's dying, he told them, meaning me.
The Border Patrol let him through.
Juan Dávila found me in pain,
the maggots in my body ate my flesh,
my dress, my hair, my teeth.
When Juan Dávila went to bury me
the ground where my body had lain was empty.
There was nothing to bury.

Juan Dávila saw pain crawling toward him.
He backed away.
Still it followed him
until he was pressed into the wall.
He watched the pain climb up his feet, legs.
When it reached his heart,
it began to eat him.
"My thoughts cause this," he cried out.
In his head he made a picture of the pain backing off,
of the pain sliding down his leg,
of the pain crawling toward the door.

Then Juan Dávila saw the pain turn around
and come back.
"If I must die, then I'll die," he said,
looking at his leg turning white.
Juan Dávila kneeled to pray.
Juan Dávila saw the pain
crawling to where my body had lain.
He saw my clothes appear,
saw my dress begin to move,
saw me sit up and open my eyes.

"You're not dead," he said.
"You prayed for me to be well," I told him.
"No, I prayed for myself," he said.
"You are everyone, when you prayed for yourself
you prayed for all of us."

Juan Dávila looked into my eyes,
saw the longing.
"You want to die, don't you," he said.
"No, I want to be with her, *la virgen santísima.*"
"But you are with her," he said,
eyes clear like a child's.
"She is everywhere."
And I heard the wind begin to blow.
As I breathed the air in and out,
I breathed her in and out.
I walked into my *jacal* to lie down,
and there on the floor by my bed
lay Juan Dávila asleep.

Get up, Juan Dávila, get in the bed.
I lay in the bed and slept.
When I woke up I saw
squirming serpents on the floor
shiny serpents on the walls
serpents moving on the windows.
A small fear appeared and entered me.
I heard a big black snake say,
"We are your healing spirit guides."
The serpents slithered off the walls
I couldn't see them anymore,
but I felt them all around me.
"What do I do now?" I asked them.

"We will teach you," they said,
"but first you must gather the herbs."

Juan Dávila and I went into the fields.
"No, this way," Juan Dávila told me.
I smiled and followed him.
We found nothing but weeds.
"*Curandera*, you knew
there were no *yerbitas* here."
"Oh, there's a few," I said.
"Look behind that big weed."
Juan Dávila bent down,
saw a tiny *romero* plant.
When he reached out to pick it
I said, "No, leave it, it's too small."
"The weeds are choking it," he said,
"and it's got no leaves."
"Help it," I told him.
"I'll go get the hoe," he said.
"No, there's no time, the plant will die.
She needs room," I said.
The weeds began to move back.
The *romero* began to grow.
The weeds moved further back.
"No, *pendejos*, let's kill her," said a big ugly *quelite*.
"No, she's so pretty," the others said,
holding him back.
The tiny *romero* grew and grew,
told them, "You're pretty too."
The weeds became long graceful grasses,
they bowed down to the *romero*.
Herbs of all kinds
poked their heads out of the earth

35

covered the fields.
I've been a *curandera*
since that day
and Juan Dávila has been my apprentice.

MIRIAM BORNSTEIN

Una pequeña contribución
1996

sneaking past that border
line of ancient smoking hearts
a rajita de chile jalapeño
landed on the other side
at home like never before

new juices came alive
dancing tongues out of control
ancient words surfacing
on white faces

rajita de chile jalapeño
le dió sabor
le dió color
al English Only

To a Linguist Studying Discourse Strategies of Bilingual/Bicultural Students
1995

On what ship did you arrive
eating apple pie
attempting to nail fifty stars
in the hearts of your Latino students?
The trade is made: linguistic examples
for bells and glass beads of assimilation,
the promise of the American Dream on a diploma.
Marking the spot with red ink
staking out new territory,
drawing new boundaries,
you say:
"These are inadmissible words;
there are disconnected ties between sentences;
need to repair, correct, or clarify discourse;
perfect written expression"
making a point
in your perfect "English Only" tongue
while presenting your claims at conferences
to sacred cows that ruminate on "Linguistic Unity"
semantic sequences detaching your heart
injecting domination into our mouths for your studies
correcting our "incoherent" expression
for your "coherent" ideology
      ephemeral   ephemeral
              slippery
              like your jargon
However, in the end
accepting our sentences to save your academic skin
you submit to our discourse.
We subvert your only tongue

and even though you use our words,
we bear no gifts
there is no stamp of ownership
upon our forehead to deliver us
no claims of property imprinted on our skin
for behind our words
we've always known a vibrant world
as ancient as the first drumbeat in the heart.

🐘 Giannina Braschi

¡Las cosas que les pasan a los hombres en Nueva York!
1986

¡Las cosas que les pasan a los hombres en Nueva York! Esto está puesto en exclamación. Es, por supuesto, una exageración—dice el narrador. No es sólo en Nueva York donde les pasan a los hombres estas cosas. Les pasan en La Habana y en Berlín. Les pasan en Madrid y en Moscú. Y no solo les pasan a los hombres. Les pasan también a las mujeres. Me pareció extraño porque no encontraba el men's room—dijo Mariquita Samper. Pregunté dónde estaba el ladies' room—dijo Uriberto Eisensweig, vestido de Berta Singerman. Luego que salí del rest room—dijo el narrador—me senté a mirar las cosas que les pasan a los hombres en Nueva York. No sé si es preciso que me cambie mi nombre. No me gusta que me llamen Mariquita Samper cuando en realidad estoy ejecutando el papel de Berta Singerman y soy una lesbiana. Maricona-Mariquita. Detrás de los bastidores Mariquita Samper se viste de Uriberto Eisensweig. Y Uriberto Eisensweig se viste de Berta Samper. ¿No sabe usted que yo soy Uriberto Singerman? ¿Y que Uriberto Samper es nada menos y nada más que Berta Eisensweig? ¡Oiga, señor, las cosas que les pasan a las mujeres en Nueva York! Mariquita: soy yo, Uriberto Eisensweig. De pronto se cae el telón. Evidentemente al público le gustan las cosas que les pasan a los hombres en Nueva York—dice el narrador. ¿Si no les gustaran estas cosas, por qué aplauden tanto? En el fondo piden que se repita la función. Aclaman mucho más a Uriberto cuando ejecuta el papel de Mariquita Samper. ¡Bravo! ¡Bravo! ¡Que se repita la función! ¡Oiga, señora, las cosas que les pasan a las mujeres en Nueva York! Ellas creen ser mujeres y son hombres. Ellos creen ser hombres y son mujeres. Tras bastidores está la madre de Mariquita Samper. No me gusta que te vistas de Uriberto. ¿Qué sacas con esto? ¿Escandalizar a la gente? Mamá. ¿No ves que están alegres? ¿No ves que se sienten felices? En el fondo de todo hombre hay una mujer. En el fondo de toda mujer hay un hombre. Las cosas son hombres y mujeres. Las manzanas buscan a las peras. Y las peras aman a los melocotones. ¡Oiga, señor, las cosas que les pasan a las peras en Nueva York! No es ninguna novedad. Ya sabemos que a los hombres les gustan las peras. Y que a los melocotones les gustan las naranjas. Ya sabemos también que la naranja es naranja. Y que la manzana es un melocotón. Eso no lo sabía—dice la mamá de la manzana.Yo creía que a mi hija le gustaban los melocotones. ¿Pero las peras? Señores, señoras—y se pone su mano sobre la cabeza. Eso no sabía que les pasaba a las mujeres en Nueva York. Señoras, señores—dice con seriedad el papá del melocotón—eso tampoco sabía que le pasaba a mi hijo. ¡Pero las cosas que les pasan a los hombres y a las mujeres!—dicen la pera y el melocotón. Incluso la manzana y la naranja. Y repiten:

¡Oh, las cosas que les pasan a los hombres en Nueva York!

¡Oh, las cosas que les pasan a las mujeres en Nueva York!

¡Bravo! ¡Bravo! FIN de esta escena.

Y FIN de otro episodio cotidiano que vivo en Nueva York.

Firma: *el narrador*

Todos dicen que es mentira la verdad. Todos dicen que es verdad la mentira. Pero yo sólo sé que estoy solo redactando una ilusión barata. Y con una lágrima en el ojo, con una lágrima que me traiciona, me río de la ironía, que me cuesta caro redactar el *Diario íntimo de la soledad*.

🐌 🐌 🐌

The Things That Happen to Men in New York!
1986

The things that happen to men in New York! This is written as an exclamation. It is, of course, an exaggeration—says the narrator. These things don't only happen in New York. They happen in Havana and Berlin. They happen in Madrid and Moscow. And they don't only happen to men. They happen to women too. I thought it was strange that I couldn't find the men's room—said Mariquita Samper. I asked where the ladies' room was—said Uriberto Eisensweig, dressed up as Berta Singerman. After I left the rest room—said the narrator—I sat down to watch the things that happen to men in New York. Maybe this is why I'm always changing my name. I don't like being called Mariquita Samper when I'm really playing Berta Singerman and I'm a lesbian. Mariquita, the Drag Queen! Mariquita Samper dresses up as Uriberto Eisensweig backstage. And Uriberto Eisensweig dresses up as Berta Samper. Don't you know that I'm Uriberto Singerman? And that Uriberto Samper is none other than Berta Eisensweig? Listen, sir, to the things that happen to men in New York! Mariquita: "It is I, Uriberto Eisensweig!" Suddenly, the curtain falls. Apparently, the public likes the things that happen to men in New York—says the narrator. Why else would they applaud so much? They're asking for an encore performance. Uriberto gets a bigger hand when he plays Mariquita Samper. Bravo! Bravo! Encore! Listen, lady, to the things that happen to women in New York! They think they're women, but they're men. They think that they're men, but they're women. Mariquita Samper's mother is backstage. I don't want you dressing up as Uriberto. What thrill do you get from scandalizing people? Mama, don't you see them laughing? Don't you see them having fun? Deep down in every man there is a woman. Deep down in every woman there is a man. Things are men and women. Apples look for pears. And pears love peaches. Listen, sir, to the things that happen to pears in New York! Nothing new. We already knew that men like pears. And that peaches like oranges. We also knew that an orange is an orange. And that an apple is a peach. I didn't know that—says the apple's mother. I thought my daughter liked peaches. But pears? Gentlemen, ladies—she says, placing her hand on her head. I didn't know that happened to women in New York. Ladies, gentlemen—says the pear's father solemnly—I didn't know that it would happen to my son. But the things that happen to men and women!—sing the pear and the peach. The apple and the orange join in the chorus:

Oh, the things that happen to men in New York!
Oh, the things that happen to women in New York!
Bravo! Bravo! THE END of this scene.
And THE END of another daily episode that I live in New York.
                                    Signed: The Narrator

Everyone says that truths are lies. Everyone says that lies are true. But I'm the only one who knows that I'm alone writing another cheap illusion. And with a tear in my eye, with a tear that gives me away, I laugh at the irony—writing *The Intimate Diary of Solitude* really takes its toll on me.

English translation by Tess O'Dwyer

Trojan Horse
1994

> *Ya llegué de donde andaba.*
> —POPULAR MEXICAN SONG

I'm a gift designed to subvert,
submerge;
sublet
the house and pretend no more
a gift that bears the power of triumphant entry

the gift that rescued
Helen or Malinche.
Ya ni sé.
Solo sé que yo no soy ni una ni la otra
but she who beyond beauty, and betrayal,
can change the world,
change her skin,
change her cover,
still,
The gift is not for all and not for always, not forever,
ni le hace si sí
o si no.

Just take my skeletal hand,
look into the eyes of night,
Come into the blinding light
Storm the fortress,

rescue those who need rescuing
offer the proper offerings

Troy or D.C. or D.F.
no le hace
The subtlest gifts come uninvited
the strongest love is unrequited.

Decolonizing the Mind
1994

First expiate all sin,
erase the lenten penance and the absolutions,
believe all miracles are fact;
accept all facts as miracles,
then expunge both fact and miracle

🐗 🐗 🐗

The needle plunges into skin and
pst, pst, pst, the germs—the bad ones—die
good invisible one, exterminator
how do you explain success?
Cancerous tumors, leukemia
erased, deleted
from the body template?
Miracle?
These are facts—the cells
rebel and immunity no longer applies.
The mind sags with the weight of
wars, of battles lost and won,
and finally loses
a Pac-Man game knows no winners.

🐗 🐗 🐗

Then erase allegiance to all flags
and feel no goose bumps at parades,
shed no tears for soldiers dead or live
See the *tricolor* and do not flinch,
the redwhiteandblue must leave you free to
marvel at the symmetry of stars,

shed not a tear, sing without quavering voice
or better still, sing a silent song.

The tongue is next. Speak only life truths
in a language yours alone.
Delete "mande" as involuntary response to your name;
Make your name your own, neither Catholic saint
nor telenovela fad.
Let words come as they must
and as a neurosurgeon might
precision-cut the words that oppress,
that control, words bad and good
that enslave and hinder,
manacles of the colonized mind.

Next, let decolonizing mist into the brain cells
where blood knows no allegiance
except its own capillaries
betrayal by memory banks closed forever,
bloodletting, leeches, close up synapses
and collapse the truth.

🐚 🐚 🐚

And finally, believe that all is not
and that nothing is
even the yellow explosion of forsythia
against early spring snow.
Colonized minds only know
the colonizers' joy.

Finally, treat tenderly
Beware the void remaining,
for nature loves a vacuum.

ANA CASTILLO

You Are Real as Earth, y Más
1990

I
A green chile ristra
you are, 'manito—
hung upside down,
on a rustic porch.
Rock, you are,
coyote, roadrunner,
scorpion stung
still running strong. Sometimes,
you are a red ristra
into whom I take burning bites
and always yearn for one
more
bite.
You are real as earth, y más.
You are air and sky. While I—
who have traveled so far to reach you,
remain the blood of fertility,
fear of your mortality,
pungent waters in which
you believe, you will surely
die a godless death.

II
And when you are not sky,
nor warm rain,
nor dust or a pebble in my shoe,

you are the smoke
of an old curandera's cigar
trailing throughout my rooms.
You are the Warrior Monkey
in a Chinese Buddhist tale; you are
copper and gold filigree—
Tlaquepaque glass blown
into the vague shape of a man,
a jaguar, a gnat. I
look for signs to see if it is really you.
Tonantzín appears as Guadalupe
on a burnt tortilla.
Coffee grounds, wax, an egg dropped
into a clear jar of water.
I look for signs everywhere.

III

I have lit farolitos to guide
you back to my door.
Turned upside down by desire,
it seems your feet
are on a groundless path. Beware of the Trickster.
The road in either direction
is neither longer nor shorter,
nor more narrow nor wider
than the fear that closes your heart.
Grey ash sediment in my entrails,
this path of ours is Sacred Ground.

Ixtacihuatl Died in Vain

1986

I

Hard are the women of my family,
hard on the mothers who've died on us
and the daughters born to us,
hard on all except sacred husbands
and the blessings of sons.
We are Ixtacihuatls,
sleeping, snowcapped volcanoes
buried alive in myths
princesses with the name of a warrior
on our lips.

II

You, my impossible bride,
at the wedding where our mothers
were not invited,
our fathers, the fourteen
stations of the cross—

You, who are not my bride,
have loved too vast, too wide.
Yet I dare to steal you
from your mother's house.

It is you
I share my son with
to whom I offer up
his palpitating heart
so that you may breathe,
and replenish yourself,
you alone, whom I forgive.

III

Life is long enough
to carry all things
to their necessary end. So
if I am with you
only this while,
or until our hair goes white,
our mothers have died,
children grown,
their children been born,
or when you spy someone
who is me
but with fresh eyes that see
you as Coatlícue once did—
and my heart
shrivels with vanity;
or a man takes me out to dance
and I leave you at the table
ice melting in your glass;
or all the jasmine in the world
has lost its scent,
let us place this born of us
at Ixtacihuatl's grave:
a footnote in the book of myths
sum of our existence—
"Even the greatest truths
contain the tremor of a lie."

*The legend of the twin volcanoes, Popocatepetl and Ixtacihuatl, in Puebla, Mexico, has it
that these were once a warrior and a princess of rival tribes who came to an end similar to
that of the two lovers in Shakespeare's Romeo and Juliet.*

Someone Told Me
1985

> *Gracias a la vida que me ha dado tanto*
> *me dió dos luceros que cuando los abro*
> *perfecto distingo, lo negro del blanco*
> —V.P.

Someone told me the other night,
over Flor de Caña rum and listening
to her records, that Violeta Parra
killed herself.
She put a gun to her head
at midnight.
All the neighbors came running
at the sound of the report.
It had something to do with economics
and the desertion of her young lover
for a woman half her age. There was
talk of jealous scenes.
Violeta Parra, who composed "Gracias
a la vida," killed herself.
Liberals and políticos might be
disappointed in this account. That
she did not die beneath the blows
of rifle butts or by electric shock,
and instead, died the death
of a woman.

In My Country
1985

This is not my country.
In my country, men
do not play at leaders
women do not play at men
there is no god
crucified to explain
the persistence of cruelty.

In my country
i don't hesitate to sit
alone in the park, to go
to the corner store at night
for my child's milk, to wear
anything that shows my breasts.

In my country
i do not stand for cutbacks,
layoffs, and pay union dues
companies do not close down
to open up again in far-off
places where eating is the
main objective.

In my country
men do not sleep with guns
beneath their pillows. They
do not accept jobs building weapons.
They don't lose their mortgages, pensions,
their faith or their dignity.

In my country
children are not abused

beaten into adulthood
left with sitters who resent them
for the meager salary a single parent
can afford. They do not grow up
to repeat the pattern.

In my country
i did not wait in line for milk
coupons for my baby, get the wrong
prescription at the clinic, was not
forced to give my ethnic origin,
nor died an unnatural death.

In my country, i am not exotic.
i do not have Asian eyes. i
was not raised on a reservation.
i do not go artificially blonde.
The sun that gravitates to my dark
pigmentation is not my enemy.

i do not watch television, entertain
myself at commercial movie houses,
invest in visual art or purchase
literature at grocery stores.

In my country, i do not stand
for the cold because i can't
afford the latest gas hike. i
am not expected to pay taxers
three times over.

This is not my world
In my world, Mesoamerica
was a magnificent Quetzal,

Africa and its inhabitants
were left alone. Arab women
don't cover their faces or
allow their sexual parts to be
torn out. In my world,
no one is prey.

Death is not a relief.
i don't bet on reincarnation
or heaven, or lose the present
in apathy or oblivion.

i do not escape into my sleep.
Analysts are not made rich by
my discoveries therein. My
mother is not cursed for giving
birth. i am not made ashamed
for being.

In my world, i do not attend
conferences with academicians
who anthropologize my existence,
dissect the simplicity of greed,
and find the differences created
out of Babel interesting.

In my world
i am a poet
who can rejoice in the coming of
Halley's comet, the wonders
of Machu Picchu, and a sudden kiss.

In my world, i breathe clean air.
i don't anticipate nuclear war.

i speak all languages. i don't
negate aging, listen to myths
to explain my misery or create them.

In my world the poet sang loud
and clear and everyone heard
without recoiling. It was sweet
as harvest, sharp as tin, strong
as the northern wind, and all had
a coat warm enough to bear it.

❧ ROSEMARY CATACALOS

A Silk Blouse
1989, 1996

> *Mérida, Yucatán, México, 1919*
> *San Antonio, Texas, EUA, 1919–1975*
> *Mérida, Yucatán, México, 1975*

The way slivers of light shift and are sifted
through narrow gaps in tropical leaves,
just so, a young woman's life is winnowed:
her love, her future separated

from her past, as if one were light and one
shadow. But which is which, and who's
to say? Her leather trunks and wicker
valises are still full of promise.

How can she know she will never marry
the man whose letters already yellow
in the folds of her new clothes? That the silk
she plans to save for him, for her

return, will end up playtime rags
for a grandchild in another country.
Our lives are this arbitrary, this much
given to chance. A father and daughter

visit her married sister north of the border.
The father leaves his youngest
in the sister's care on foreign soil
to marry his chosen kindly stranger.

A father's right to keep her from ruin,
the wrong man at home. Papa's boat
hangs at the port like a scythe. The silk,
the letters, grow thin with tears and touching.

Years pass, and life with the kindly
stranger grows its own story.
Their days are sad and happy like everyone's.
She lives things the way they are.

Today a friend asks, *Who is she
and what is she to you?* It should
be simple to say she was my grandmother,
one of the ways I'm here to speak

of light sifting through tropical trees.
But what is simple, even now?
The man she loved was called Miguel.
On our last visit to Mérida

a few months before she died,
she introduced me to an old man
who kept a hardware stall in the market,
scissors, knives, a few curios.

He gave me an *henequén* bag painted
with Mayan scenes, and I recalled my games
with the silk, how the shadows played on it,
the light. How I made up other lives.

At Home in the World

for Beverly Lowry
1988

The dream is of something coming. Growing
as the heart does in love, inevitably
bent on its own motion, a sunflower turning
a ripe face toward its source.
The dream is of something possible and regular,
the silence of an old man husking pinenuts
in a whitewashed courtyard at sunset, the fading
light: memory become dream again.

The dream is pure necessity. For what
are the givens if not that we give everything,
whatever it takes? There are bombs
in innocent places. Old friends grow tired
and want to die. The night-blooming
cereus is doused in its one moment
of fire. A storm carries away
trucks full of children mouthing questions.
It can strike anywhere, this life.

Which is why we are hard on its heels, saying
always, *If these things are true, then so
is the dream.* Why we hold the dream out
like some mismatched gift, but a gift
even so. For a grandmother who remembers
its name, for a little boy straining
on tiptoe to see into a snow-filled park.

Insufficient Light

for Thanasis Maskeleris
1990

Under the stairs, the light is going faster
  than in the courtyard where Yianni strikes
   sand from the hems of his trousers and only
    that briefly knows the woman is weeping
     in the shadows, that her tears are partly his
      doing, that the light's going is not, but is
       somehow related.

Dusk catches in the crook of her elbow,
  in the sleeve she raises to wipe her face,
   embracing odors of fish, basil, roses hard won
    from rocky soil. But now the sand is off
     his clothes, Yianni turns away,
      demands the coffee be set to boil,
       their little bread divided.

Years later Yianni sits alone in the courtyard
  at dusk. Gazing at a cat near the boats,
   he suddenly recalls how the woman wept and is
    confused by the terrible bellow that rises
     out of him, the way he smashes his cane against
      the whitewashed wall under the stairs, his wanting
       to stroke her hair in the going light.

Morning Geography

for Naomi Shihab Nye
1993

Suppose the flower rioting on my desk, an exotic shout of yellow
streaked with red, ruffled as an agitated jungle bird,

suppose this flower, large as my hand, could be pulled apart
and the sweetness wrung out the way we did honeysuckle so long

ago on heavy summer nights with fireflies: This drop of honey
for courage, this drop of honey for love, this drop for anything

you are dreaming of. . . . Last night I dreamed a woman I love
(in Spanish we say dreamed with, *soñé con* Noemi) running furiously

through Texas sagebrush to save her Uncle Mohammed, who died
on a mountain in Palestine years ago, a hermit who wanted no saving.

Dreams are like this, make all things possible. The way just now,
still drugged with sleep, I supposed a loud flower could save us, tell us

something about sweetness when half a world away a man tends a fire
in the street before his tiny rug shop, a short distance from some broken

buildings. He breathes the dense air of burning tires, decoy smoke
to make the bombers think they've already struck here. Suppose we could

have coffee with him, strong, laced with cardamom and small talk.
Suppose we'd figured out, on those immense and long ago

lost summer nights how to get at the sweetness
without tearing the proud throat of even one blossom.

Beneath the Shadow
of the Freeway
1975

1
Across the street—the freeway,
blind worm, wrapping the valley up
from Los Altos to Sal Si Puedes.
I watched it from my porch
unwinding. Every day at dusk
as Grandma watered geraniums
the shadow of the freeway lengthened.

2
We were a woman family:
Grandma, our innocent Queen;
Mama, the Swift Knight, Fearless Warrior.
Mama wanted to be Princess instead.
I know that. Even now she dreams of taffeta
and foot-high tiaras.

Myself: I could never decide.
So I turned to books, those staunch, upright men.
I became Scribe: Translator of Foreign Mail,
interpreting letters from the government, notices
of dissolved marriages and Welfare stipulations.
I paid the bills, did light man-work, fixed faucets,
insured everything
against all leaks.

3
Before rain I notice seagulls.
They walk in flocks,
cautious across lawns: splayed toes,
indecisive beaks. Grandma says
seagulls mean storm.
In California in the summer,
mockingbirds sing all night.
Grandma says they are singing for their nesting wives.
"They don't leave their families
borrachando."

She likes the ways of birds,
respects how they show themselves
for toast and a whistle.

She believes in myths and birds.
She trusts only what she builds
with her own hands.

4
She built her house,
cocky, disheveled carpentry,
after living twenty-five years
with a man who tried to kill her.

Grandma, from the hills of Santa Barbara,
I would open my eyes to see her stir mush
in the morning, her hair in loose braids,
tucked close around her head
with a yellow scarf.

Mama said, "It's her own fault,
getting screwed by a man for that long.

Sure as shit wasn't hard."
soft she was soft

5
in the night I would hear it
glass bottles shattering the street
words cracked into shrill screams
inside my throat   a cold fear
as it entered the house in hard
unsteady steps   stopping at my door
my name   bathrobe   slippers
outside a 3 A.M. mist heavy
as a breath full of whiskey
stop   it go home   come inside
mama if he comes here again
I'll call the police

inside
a gray kitten   a touchstone
purring beneath the quilts
grandma stitched
from his suits
the patchwork singing
of mockingbirds

6
"You're too soft . . . always were.
You'll get nothing but shit.
Baby, don't count on nobody."
—a mother's wisdom.
Soft. I haven't changed,
maybe grown more silent, cynical
on the outside.

"O Mama, with what's inside of me
I could wash that all away. I could."

"But, Mama, if you're good to them
they'll be good to you back."

Back. The freeway is across the street.
It's summer now. Every night I sleep with a gentle man
to the hymn of mockingbirds,

and in time, I plant geraniums.
I tie up my hair into loose braids,
and trust only what I have built
with my own hands.

Bird Ave
1985

life on Bird
was tough
Cat-eyes
me and Mousie
estrolándonos y
marchando
con missions
man I can't get no
satisfaction
in and out las
baby baby baby
oooo OOO oooo
baby baby
hits all summer

we wore tease
tight skirts
tough teased hair
talked tough rhymes
developed una
re-puta-ción
for the toughest burns
on Horseshoe

tough
from Memorial Day
to our Labor Day
weekend
we had the key
to the drug locker
of our own developing

temples
highest kites in the district
favors all over town
and we owed
nobody shit

Cat-eyes was beautiful
Mouse made up wizard holds
nobody over 4'11" could contain her
except me—the connection
we always had it
we scored
when we wanted
plus we were ethical

essssahhh Mouse goes
that first initiation
you gotta understand
about Ethics
she had it then
all total control
banging my head on
the blacktop for effect
you flacafeaface
got Ethics
and she gave me
one of those mouse
grins and made
lemon crap
out of my cheeks
before letting me up
all righteous rage

sin class *ni* pomp
and circumstance

we were better
than military
beauty brains & brass
man
we were the trinity
that invented it
the model rambos
I coulda killed her
easy
she knew it
we'd kill it
in ourselves
eventually

we knew it all
the code and the symbology
the poetics and the order
of place and gesture
we were honed for the killing
primed for the time
our *ganga de* camelias
y rosarías would burst
we tended that bust
cultivated it
blistered it
hitched ourselves
up to its hearse
and made up Bird
on the reins
of some wild ride
from the tracks to
Willow Glen and back
we were running
our own private
miracle mile

man
it was tough
with Cat-eyes
on the corner
buttering 'em up
all stupid and blind
me and Mouse
always ready
to take advantage
of a relevant situation

Don't Fuck With Us
our motto
We're Here to Serve
the ruse
Listen Watch
Be Silent
was the Conquest's
hidden code

man
it was tough
to know it all
and we haven't
learned anything
since

On Love and Hunger
1986

I feed you
as you hunger.
I hunger
as you feed
and refuse
the food I give.

Hunger is the first sense.
Imagination is the last.
You are my sixth sense,
imaginary lover,
missed meal.

Food is first choice,
first flaw, fatal
in its accessibility,
fearless on the tongue
of mean denial.

First word.
First sight.

Food is love
in trust.

Emplumada
1980

When summer ended
the leaves of snapdragons withered
taking their shrill-colored mouths with them.
They were still, so quiet. They were
violet where umber now is. She hated
and she hated to see
them go. Flowers

born when the weather was good—this
she thinks of, watching the branch of peaches
daring their ways above the fence, and further,
two hummingbirds, hovering, stuck to each other,
arcing their bodies in grim determination
to find what is good, what is
given them to find. These are warriors

distancing themselves from history.
They find peace
in the way they contain the wind
and are gone.

Lápiz Azul
1981

A blast of the bluest
air—my jay sears
across free clouds
with sheer audacity.
I love you like this.
A swoop of the heart
and there it is—a field
so blue I live through
a dense dream of wet
and white. This world
could be a dream, this
dream, a universe.
This season's flight
I go, holding an in-
efficient compass
of pure heart. Love,
I can't tell you
how it is to dissolve
out of duty and air
and the thick grief
of the expendable.

🐦 LISA CHÁVEZ

The Crow's Bride
1995

> *I have written a true statement of my captivity; what I suffered and*
> *what I was spared from suffering, by a Friendly or Christian*
> *Indian. . . . I trust that the world will not censure me for speaking*
> *kindly of those who saved me from death and dishonor.*
>   —SARAH F. WAKEFIELD,
>   *Six Weeks in the Sioux Tepees,*
>   1863

I dreamed of the crow, sooty ravisher
of gardens, scavenger, but in dreams tame,
familiar, a kindred soul. Chaska.
His name, like harsh cry of crow.

Waking, my face wet with tears. Why
must I remember, again and
again, why these tears, bitter
as the blood—so much—that watered
the earth that summer. So long ago,
my captivity. Chaska. Of him and me
so many evil things were said:
that I wished him spared
because I loved him. I could not
love a savage, though I could respect one.
The day the massacre began, who was there
to save me? Who heard the war whoops,
Hapa's drunken laugh as he pointed
his gun, my neighbor Gleason's body slumping
into mine, his chest a bloody bowl.
The rifle's swivel towards me.

Chaska's intervention. Who but me saw,
smelled, the burning farms, the broken
bodies, a feast for flies. All this
he saved me from. And why? A remembered kindness
from me, the doctor's wife.

My own people were so long—oh, so long!—
in coming. Where were they as I huddled
in the heat and stench of Chaska's tepee
of ill-cured hides, my babes curled around me.
I did not love him. Could not, him a savage: fierce
bird gaze, dusky skin, hair long
and dark as a winter's night. His caresses
I would have borne, nonetheless, if my babes
be saved. But he did not caress. Morning
after morning, I woke to the sun, steaming
us awake, the drone of flies, his unblinking
gaze. Only once did he touch me,
the night Hapa reached for me, eyes mad
with whiskey. Chaska rose, his shadow
covering me like a blanket. "I will take her
for myself." Hapa demanded proof.
Even the smoke froze, suspended in the air.
Then gently as the leaf falls, he slid between
me and my babes, laid at my side. Fire
whispered, the children's sleeping moans
stilled, Chaska's breath spiced sage
near my face. His hand on my hip. Satisfied,
Hapa departed, and Chaska slipped away
to his bed across the fire. Beside me
the earth turned sweet.

So when the tribunal said Chaska should
hang for the murder Hapa committed, is it any wonder

I screamed those words? "Captain Grant, if you hang
that man, I will shoot you." In my passion
for justice, I said that, though my words
fluttered uselessly away, like my reputation, lost
in the storm of accusations: Indian lover,
adulterer, whore. All that I bore.
They hanged him by accident,
so they said, his pardon forgotten. And my habit
of tears began. An Indian wife would have painted
her face with ash, torn her hair, her clothes.
I did not. When I received news
of Chaska's death, my husband
Dr. Wakefield was drunk. Seeing my tears,
he beat me, left my face stained
with bruise. Tears proof of my guilt.
Whore. Such was my life
before my captivity. And after.

Chaska they hung because of me,
that I dared defend him guilt enough.
The last time I saw him, chained, he asked
why I had forsaken him, reminded me
how he'd sold his coat for flour
to feed me, how he'd saved my life.
I could not save him, though I tried.
Even his poor body, I could not
save, dug up a year later by white men
who took his scalp. You can see it,
at the historical society, his fine
crow-colored hair fading
before the curious stares. As for me,
you see how it is. An old woman, reviled
by my own kind. My husband dead, a suicide.
My children scattered. Myself, memory ridden.

Over the hanging ground, a Dakota woman tells me,
thirty-eight eagles circle, souls of the dead.
Eagles. I wonder. For again and again, I dream
of the crow, so familiar, so dear.
I did not love him. Across the fire's ashes,
in the dark of those hot and terrible
nights, he did not touch me. And yet
I dream of him still. Chaska. I am twice
widowed. Mourning, in black I dress.
The crow's bride.

Wild Horses
1987

I remember
when I was fourteen
and Papa caught me
sneaking out to meet
that hot-blooded ranch hand
from Pine Lake.

He beat me good.
Said he was beating out
my wild Indian blood.
Mama never said a word
but watched him
with dark berry eyes.
Papa told me
Louisa, a woman
has two choices
in this world—
wife or whore.
You had best
remember that.

My sister Charlotte
dreamed of being a wife
from the time she could
walk. She married a white man,
had three babies
in four years.
And I dreamed
of wild horses.

I remember
what it felt like

to be young
to be as fresh
and new as green wood.
I remember
riding my pony across
hot summer fields
with strangers and coming
back with lovers.

I loved white boys.
Tom, the ranch hand,
had hair as fair
as winter wheat.
At eighteen, he was half
man, half boy.
His arms were smooth
as river stones.

I loved Indian boys
who smelled of rain
and woodsmoke.
I remember
that Archambault boy.
He brought me gifts
of wild geese
and venison.

I married
a Blackfoot man
whose skin was warm
and brown as the earth
we lived on. I loved
the way he smelled—
clean and wild
as a young horse.

Now I am alone.
I sit by my stove
drinking coffee
with three sugars
and baking pies
for my grandchildren.
And I laugh.
I laugh because
Papa was wrong.
No one cares
what I was like then.
No one else remembers.

You Bring Out the Mexican in Me
1992

You bring out the Mexican in me.
The hunkered thick dark spiral.
The core of a heart howl.
The bitter bile.
The tequila lágrimas on Saturday all
through next weekend Sunday.
You are the one I'd let go the other loves for,
surrender my one-woman house.
Allow you red wine in bed,
even with my vintage lace linens.
Maybe. Maybe.

For you.

You bring out the Dolores del Rio in me.
The Mexican spitfire in me.
The raw *navajas*, glint and passion in me.
The raise Cain and dance with the rooster-footed devil in me.
The spangled sequin in me.
The eagle and serpent in me.
The *mariachi* trumpets of the blood in me.
The Aztec love of war in me.
The fierce obsidian of the tongue in me.
The *berrinchuda, bien-cabrona* in me.
The Pandora's curiosity in me.
The pre-Columbian death and destruction in me.
The rain-forest disaster, nuclear threat in me.

The fear of fascists in me.
Yes, you do. Yes, you do.

You bring out the colonizer in me.
The holocaust of desire in me.
The Mexico City '85 earthquake in me.
The Popocatepetl/Ixtacihuatl in me.
The tidal wave of recession in me.
The Agustín Lara hopeless romantic in me.
The *barbacoa taquitos* on Sunday in me.
The cover the mirrors with cloth in me.

Sweet twin. My wicked other,
I am the memory that circles your bed nights,
that tugs you taut as moon tugs ocean.
I claim you all mine,
arrogant as Manifest Destiny.
I want to rattle and rend you in two.
I want to defile you and raise hell.
I want to pull out the kitchen knives,
dull and sharp, and whisk the air with crosses.
Me sacas lo mexicana en mi,
like it or not, honey.

You bring out the Uled-Nayl in me.
The stand-back-white-bitch in me.
The switchblade in the boot in me.
The Acapulco cliff diver in me.
The *Flecha Roja* mountain disaster in me.
The dengue fever in me.
The *¡Alarma!* murderess in me.
I could kill in the name of you and think
it worth it. Brandish a fork and terrorize rivals,

female and male, who loiter and look at you,
languid in your light. Oh,

I am evil. I am the filth goddess Tlazoltéotl.
I am the swallower of sins.
The lust goddess without guilt.
The delicious debauchery. You bring out
the primordial exquisiteness in me.

The nasty obsession in me.
The corporal and venial sin in me.
The original transgression in me.

Red ocher. Yellow ocher. Indigo. Cochineal.
Piñón. Copal. Sweetgrass. Myrrh.
All you saints, blessed and terrible,
Virgen de Guadalupe, diosa Coatlícue,
I invoke you.

Quiero ser tuya. Only yours, Only you.
Quiero amarte. Atarte. Amarrarte.
Love the way a Mexican woman loves. Let
me show you. Love the only way I know how.

With Lorenzo at the Center of the Universe, el Zócalo, Mexico City
1989

We had to cross the street twice
because of rats. But there it was.
The *zócalo* at night and la Calle de la Moneda
like a dream out of Canaletto. Forget
Canaletto. This was real.

And you were there, Lorenzo.
The cathedral smoky-eyed and still
rising like a pyramid after all
these centuries. You named the four
holy centers—Amecameca, Tepeyac, and two
others I can't remember. I remember you,
querida flecha, and how all the words I knew
left me. The ones in English and the few
in Spanish too.

This is the center of the universe,
I said and meant it. This is eternity.
This moment. Now. And love,
that wisp of copal that scared the hell
out of you when I mentioned it,
love is eternal, though
what eternity has to do with tomorrow,
I don't know. Understand?

I'm not sure you followed me.
Not now, not then. But I know
what I felt when I put my hand
on your heart, and there was that kiss,
just that, from the center of the universe.
Or at least my universe.

Lorenzo, is the center of the universe
always so lonely at night and so
crowded in the day? Earlier
I'd been birthed from the earth
when the metro bust loose at noon.
Stumbled up the steps over Bic pens
embroidered with Batman logos, red
extension cords, vinyl wallets, velveteen
roses, pumpkin seed vendors, brilliant
masons looking for work. I remember the boy
with the burnt foot carried by his mother,
the smell of meat frying, a Styrofoam
plate sticky with grease.

At night we fled
the racket of Garibaldi and mariachis
chasing cars down Avenida Lázaro Cárdenas
for their next meal. At La Hermosa Hortensia,
lights bright as an ice cream parlor,
faces sweaty and creased with grief.
My first pulque warm and frothy like semen.

On the last evening we said good-bye
along two streets named after rivers. I
fumbled with the story of Borges and his Delia.
When we meet again beside what river?
But this was no poem. Only mosquitoes
biting like hell and a good-bye
kiss like a mosquito bite that left
me mad for hours. After all,
hadn't it taken centuries for us
to meet at the center of the universe
and consummate a kiss?

Lorenzo, I forget what's real.
I mix up the details of what happened
with what I witnessed inside my
universe. Is it like that for you?
But I thought for a moment, I really did,
that a kiss could be a universe.
Or sex. Or love, that old shoe. See.
Still hopeless. Still writing poems
for pretty men. Half of me alive
again. The other shouting from the sidelines,
Sit down, clown.

Ah, Lorenzo, I'm a fool.
Eternity or bust. That's how it is with me.
Even if eternity is simply one kiss,
one night, one moment. And if love isn't
eternal, what's the point?

If I knew the words I'd explain
how a man loves a woman before love
and how he loves her after
is never the same. How the two halves split
and can't be put back whole again
Isn't it a shame?

You named the holy centers but forgot
one—the heart. Said every
time you'd pass this *zócalo*
you'd think of me and that kiss
from the center of the universe.

I remember you, Lorenzo. See
this *zócalo*? Remember me.

Once Again I Prove the Theory of Relativity
1993

If
you came back
I'd treat you
like a lost Matisse
couch you like a Pasha
dance a Sevillana
leap and backflip like a Taiwanese diva
bang cymbals like a Chinese opera
roar like a Fellini soundtrack
and laugh like the little dog that
watched the cow jump over the moon

I'd be your clown
I'd tell you funny stories and
paint clouds on the walls of my house
dress the bed in its best linen
And while you slept
I'd hold my breath and watch
you move like a sunflower

How beautiful you are
like the color inside an ear
like a conch shell
like a Modigliani nude.

I'll cut a bit of your hair this time
so that you'll never leave me
Ah, the softest hair
Ah, the softest

If
you came back

I'd give you parrot tulips and papayas
laugh at your stories
Or I wouldn't say a word which,
as you know, is hard for me

I know when you grew tired
off you'd go to Patagonia
Cairo Istanbul
Katmandu
Laredo

Meanwhile
I'll have savored you like an oyster
memorized you
held you under my tongue
learned you by heart
So that when you leave
I'll write poems

❧ JUDITH ORTIZ COFER

Absolution in the New Year
1989

The decade is over, time to begin forgiving
old sins. Thirteen years since your death
on a Florida interstate—and again
a dream of an old wrong. Last night as I slept
through the turning of the year,
                              I was fifteen
and back on the day I hated you most: when
in a patriarchal fury at my sullen
keeping of myself to myself,
and convinced I was turning into a Jezebel,
you searched my room for evidence
of a secret other life. You found my diary
under the mattress and, taking it to the kitchen,
examined it under harsh light.
                              You read
about my childish fantasies of flight—yes—
from your tyrannical vigilance
and, in the last few pages, of my first love,
almost all imagination.
                              I suffered
biblical torments as you turned the pages. Unworthy,
exposed before your eyes, I wondered where
I would go, if you should cast me out
of your garden of thorns, but I swore, that day,
my faith to the inviolable self.
                              Later
when Mother came in to offer me

a cup of consolation tea, her vague justifications
of "man's ways," and to return the profaned book,
I tore and crumpled each page, and left them
on the floor for her to sweep.
To this day
I cannot leave my notebooks open anywhere:
and I hide my secrets in poems.

A new year begins.
I am almost your age. And I can almost understand
your anger then—caught as you were—in a poor man's trap,
you needed to own, at least our souls.
For this sin of pride, I absolve you, Father.

And more:
If I could travel to your grave today,
I'd take my books of poetry as an offering
to your starved spirit
that fed on my dreams in those days.

I'd place poems on your stone marker,
over the part of your name we share,
over the brief span of your years (1933–1976),
like a Chinese daughter who brings a bowl of rice
and a letter to set on fire—a message
to be delivered by the wind: Father,

here is more for you to read.
Take all you desire of my words. Read
until you've had your fill.
Then rest in peace.

There is more where this came from.

Saint Rose of Lima

1987

> *Never let my hands be to anyone*
> *an occasion for temptation.*
> —Isabel de Flores

She was the joke of the angels—a girl
crazy enough for God

that she despised her own beauty; who grew bitter herbs
to mix with her food,

who pinned a garland of roses to her forehead;
and who, in a fury of desire

concocted a potion of Indian pepper and bark
and rubbed it on her face, neck, and breasts,

disfiguring herself.
Then, locked away in a dark cell,

where no reflection was possible,
she begged for death to join her with her Master

whom she called *Divine Bridegroom, Thorn*
in My Heart, Eternal Spouse.

She would see His vague outline, feel His cool touch
on her fevered brow,

but as relief came, her vision would begin to fade,
and once again she would dip the iron bar into the coals,

and pass it gently like a magician's wand over her skin—
to feel the passion that flames for a moment,

in all dying things.

Who Will Not Be Vanquished?

—for Tanya

1988

1.

I named you for a snow-princess
in a Russian novel,
a woman of noble bearing
who would not be vanquished
by war or passion: not Lara,
the other one—the quiet aristocrat
who inspired no poems from the man
but for whom he walked the frozen miles.

2.

Gold earrings flashing
through your black hair, you pirouette
so that your wide skirt blooms
around the long stems of your legs
for me to admire your wild beauty.
You are transformed
into one of the gypsy ancestors
we have never discussed.

3.

On the fall day of your birth,
in a city not far enough north
of the equator for my fantasy,
I held on to *Doctor Zhivago*
so hard, that when the first pain came,
I broke the spine. While the hot wires
announcing your arrival shot through me,
I imagined a sleigh pulled
by strong white horses, gliding

over a landscape of powdery snow.
In the distance: an ice palace.

4.

Today you want to go somewhere exotic:
an island in the Caribbean
inhabited only by beautiful young people;
a place where a girl might pick
from anyone's garden, a red hibiscus
for her hair, and wear a dress so light
that any breeze might make it dance;
where a dark-haired man
wearing a flowered shirt
leans against the bright blue wall
of a café, holding a guitar,
waiting for inspiration.

5.

Mourning suits us Spanish women.
Tragedy turns us into Antigone—maybe
we are bred for the part.

6.

Your best friend, also fifteen,
leaped from her father's speeding car
during an argument. After the call,
I saw how your eyes darkened
as you listened to my careful words;
I saw the women of our family in black,
gathering in a circle around you.

7.

On the ride to the hospital,
you sit up straight, averting your gaze.

I place my hand on your trembling shoulder,
and assure you that it's OK to cry.
But, gently, you disengage yourself
from my intrusive touch.
Without looking back, you walk away from me,
and into the antiseptic castle where she waits
like a captive maiden in her costume of gauze.

8.
She waits there, regal in her pain, eager
to recount her wingless flight, to show you
her wounds, and to tell you
about the betrayals of parents.

❧ LUCHA CORPI

Sonata a dos voces
A Mark Greenside
1988

1. Largo Frenético
Cuesta saberse viva
en la actividad inaudita
de estos días.

Se congregan parvadas de semanas
domingos llenos de números
jueves quiméricos
en los que el tiempo
se traiciona a sí mismo
y regresa a la hora cero.

Tanto que combatir:
mensajes a la puerta
reuniones
fechas
nombres sumergidos
en un mar de sudor
mercaderías
sopa
habas frescas
y ropa sucia

Tejemanejes que desenredar
que remendar camisas
deshilar ausencias

y neutralizar bichos burócratas
para recobrar aquellos sueños
que quedaron en el empeño
cuando se ajustó el presupuesto
y el amigo partió sin decir palabra,
cuando hubo que plantar jacintos
en las tumbas de nuestros muertos.

2. Adagio
Se me ha clavado un silencio en la garganta
un cúmulo de voz coagulada que tenaz impide
todo deseo de canto.

Los ojos apuran el crepúsculo
en sorbos verdemente lentos
y la palabra queda entrelabios
como un débil aroma a jazmines muertos.

Por la calle
alguien silba una tonado taciturna
se detiene y recoge los últimos tréboles
de la temporada
para la hija pequeña en casa
que gusta todavía
de estos diminutos prodigios
la que comparte el sueño del ciempiés
de recorrer el mundo a pie frenético
algun día.

En el patio
el limonero ha dado flor y fruto
entre mil balas de lluvia
y la violencia del viento.

A lo lejos
el tren zumba rumbo al sur
y a galope tendido la niebla lo acompaña.

Estupefacta
la ciudad contempla su perfil
en el espejo pérfido del agua
mientras
en El Salvador los niños mueren de prisa
y en África la sangre se seca lenta
y no hay palabra que pueda detener
el largo beso de sombras de la muerte
si no se extiende la mano amiga
si el corazón permanece ajeno
porque
a fin de cuentas
solamente el amor nos salva.

Sonata in Two Voices
To Mark Greenside
1989

1. **Largo Frenético**
    It's hard to realize I'm alive
    in the improbable rush
    of these days.

    Weeks accumulate in droves
        Sundays full of numbers
        chimerical Thursdays
        when time
        betrays itself
        and returns to zero hour.

    So many fronts to fight on:
        messages at the door
        meetings
        dates
        names submerged
        in a sea of sweat
        shopping lists
        soup
        fresh lima beans
        and dirty clothes

Schemes to straighten out
shirts to mend
absences to unravel
bureaucratic bugs to neutralize
before we can recover the dreams
we left in the pawnshop
when our budget got tighter

and a friend left without a word,
when the time came to plant hyacinths
on the graves of our dead.

2. **Adagio**
   A silence is embedded in my throat
   a clot of voice stubbornly blocking
   any desire to sing.

   My eyes drink the dusk
   in slow green draughts
   and words linger between my lips
   like the fading scent of dead jasmine.

   In the street
   someone is whistling a quiet tune
   stopping to gather the last clover
   of the season
   for a little daughter at home
   who still likes
   these small wonders
   and shares the centipede's dream
   of roaming the world on frantic feet
   one day.

   In the patio
   amid a thousand bullets of rain
   and violent wind
   the lemon tree has bloomed and borne fruit.

   In the distance
   a train rumbles southward
   the fog moving with it at full gallop.

Stupefied
the city gazes at its profile
in the faithless mirror of the water
while
in El Salvador children die quickly
and in Africa the blood dries slowly
and there is no word that can avert
the long, shadowed kiss of death
if no friendly hand reaches out
if the heart remains a stranger
because
when all is said and done
only love will save us.

English translation by Catherine Rodríquez-Nieto

Plaza
1989

Solitaria ahora

Llena de niebla

Las gaviotas
naves fantasmas de guerra
entre la bruma

Los faroles
testigos mudos
de batallas
que no cuentan
los libros de historia

Sangre
y despojos
pisoteados
por perros vagabundos
cronistas
de lo inmencionable

Una chicana
escoba en mano
desde la alcaldía
percibe el ascenso
de la *Júpiter* de Mozart
ensancha el alma
y atrapa una estrella.

Town Square
1989

Deserted now

Full of mist

The seagulls
phantom warships
in the fog

The streetlights
mute witnesses
of battles
never to be recounted
in history books

Blood
and human remains
trampled
by wandering dogs
chroniclers
of the unspeakable

From the town hall
a Chicana
broom in hand
hears the ascending chords
of Mozart's *Jupiter*
her soul opens
she catches a star.

English translation by Catherine Rodríguez-Nieto

Recuerdo íntimo
Para Arturo y Finnigan
1986

No había llovido así
desde aquel día en que los perros
destrozaron los únicos zapatos que tenías
y mi bolsa estaba llena solamente
de papeles y palabras.

Llovía tanto aquella tarde
que Finnigan el gato, tú y yo,
a falta de arca, decidimos meternos
a la tina de baño, por si acaso . . .

Esta tarde llueve igual que entonces
pero mi razón se niega a reandar
aquel infame invierno:
Sólo escucho la lluvia en el tejado,
el ronroneo del gato en la tina de baño,
veo la suave luz de tu sonrisa de dos años.

Es todo lo que necesito recorder.

Intimate Memory

For Arturo and Finnigan
1986

It hadn't rained like that
since the day the dogs
ruined the only shoes you had
and papers and words
were all there was in my purse.

It rained so hard that afternoon
that Finnigan the cat and you and I
decided, for want of an ark, to climb into
the bathtub, just in case . . .

It's raining again like that this afternoon
but the rational part of me refuses to go back
to that wretched winter:
I only hear the rain on the roof
and the cat purring in the bathtub,
see the soft light of your two-year-old's smile.

That's all I need to remember.

Enlish translation by Catherine Rodríquez-Nieto

❧ SILVIA CURBELO

Photograph of My Parents
1994

I like the way they look together
and how simply her smile floats towards him
out of the dim afterglow

of some memory, his hand
cupped deliberately
around the small flame

of a match. In this light
nothing begins or ends
and the camera's pale eye

is a question that answers itself
in the asking. *Are you there?*
And they are. Behind them

the wind tears down and blows
apart, angel of nonchalance.
The world belongs to the world.

For years he smoked down to the filters
sorting out the pieces of his life
with the insomniac's penchant

for detail. In the heart's
heavy forest, the tree of self-denial,
the bough, the single leaf

like the blade of a word held back
for a long time. The moment
she leans towards him the room

will become part of the story.
The light is still as a pond.
My mother's blue scarf

is the only wave.

Balsero *Singing*

1995

When he opens his mouth
he is drifting, he is
in the air, and the child

he's remembering leans out
of some dark window
in his head. The sunlight

is incidental, falling
all around him like a word
or a wing. In another dream

he is dancing in a cottage by the sea
and music is a language he has just
learned to speak, the cool *yes*

of her throat. The sky goes on
for days with its one cloud waving,
the song lifting him like a sail.

The real boat is lost
at sea, one voice nailed
to the planks of history, salt

on the tongue of thirty years.
A window empties
its small cargo—

an eyelash, grief. Each new breath
is a harbor, then a wave
closes over it

like a book.

If You Need a Reason

—for Adrian

1993

The way things move sometimes,
light or air,
the distance between
two points, or a map unfolding
on a table, or wind,
never mind sadness.
The difference between sky and room,
between geometry and breath,
the sound we hear
when two opposites finally collide,
smashed bottle, country song,
a bell, any bridge, a connection.
The way some stories end in the middle
of a word,
the words themselves,
galaxies, statuaries, perspectives,
the stone over stone that is life,
never mind hunger.
The way things move, road,
mirror, blind luck. The way
nothing moves sometimes,
a kiss, a glance,
never mind true north.
The difference between history
and desire, between biology
and prayer, any light
to read by, any voice at the bottom
of the stairs, or the sound
of your own name softly, a tiny bone
breaking near the heart.

❧ Angela de Hoyos *p 307*

La Vie: I Never Said It Was Simple
for Alicia Z. Galván—3/27/96
1996

She reminds me of that painting by
Velázquez: *La Infanta Margarita,*
in a pink and silver gown . . .

except that here, she is sentadita muy
atenta, listening to my incantations,
listening as I command the heavens,
cutting the clouds con mi cuchillito;

eyes round with hope in breathless
expectation, she wants simple clear-cut
answers to her square-root questions;

little does she know I can barely—just
barely—hew my own antidotal sword
from the selfsame tree that grows the
nightmare dragons. (. . . Ay, if only I had
the wisdom of Sor Juana!)

. . . An oracle? Listen, I am nowhere *near*
Delphi. Ni soy curandera, con polvitos y
milagros, con monitos de aserrín

. . . not a wonder-woman-shaman who
paints a mystic mandala, who wraps up the
world in a huge tortilla de maíz, with a
     Here it is, take it, it's all yours.

. . . She is, let us say, a captive voyeur
witnessing the secret dragline of my
voice. My voice that comes and goes like
the wail of La Llorona . . . Llora que llora

La Llorona . . . ¿Por sus hijos? . . . Ay, no . . .
Llora porque *nunca* tuvo hijos. Pobrecita,
es yerma. Qué pena. So she cries and cries.
Llora que llora La Llorona por los callejones
de San Cuilmas. Finally, por fin, she comes
to her favorite stomping ground: the river.
She finds her spic & span spot on a rock,
sits down and dries her eyes con una pata.
A sigh, and she twists her thorax to the right,
reaches down to open the tiny silver door of
her spinneret. Out comes the moonlight magic.
The magic moonlight thread. The moonlight
thread with which she weaves her stories. Her
brain-children. Her bambinos. Los muñecos y
las monadas:
       Míos. Re-te-míos. Re-que-te-míos! Just
think! Such beautiful 8-legged people. . . .

And she thinks and thinks and thinks about it,
until she imagines they are in truth her very
own. (The people, that is—and well yes, the
stories too. . . . Why, everyone knows she puts
them to bed every night, singing a soft
       Coo-coo-roo-coo-coo paloma
. . . all dressed up in pink & blue & yellow
pajamas. Pink for girls. Blue for boys. And yellow
for those undecided.)

. . . But let's not talk about chiquilladas. Let's talk
instead about that sword—yeah, sure, why not—

that Huitzilopochtli sword of lightning. If we
follow the *HOW-TO* instructions carefully, I'm
sure we can construct one. . . . Oh, yes, of course,
someone is *bound* to discover our upstart
"Wishing Well" machinations. Our Mad Hatter;
our Crazy Coyotl notions. . . .

But by then, it will be too late. I will have given
you the sword. You will have given it to the Queen.
The Queen has called a meeting of the deck. The
deck has counted the ayes and the nays. Meeting
adjourned!!! The order has been submitted in
triplicate. Sealed and delivered by hand. At 10 A.M.,
the Queen accepts and *HO!* . . . A deft swing, a
ringing whoooooosh . . . and there!!! She has klopt
off the eeny meany, what a greedy Medusa head. . . .

¿Ya ves? Like I said, it's not simple . . .

La Malinche a Cortés y Vice Versa
(o sea, "El Amor No Perdona, Ni Siquiera Por Amor")
1979

ELLA: Dame tu nombre, mi amo y señor,
para que me adorne. Cómo quisiera
grabarlo aquí, junto con el mío
en la arena. Es que soy tuya
y quiero que lo sepa
todo el mundo.

EL: Todo el mundo
ya lo sabe,
mi querida Marina. No necesitas
adornos superfluos.
Yo te quiero y eso basta.

Y entre paréntesis EL se dijo:

Además, ¡¡¡hrrrmmmppp!!! Es indigno
que un hombre blanco
de mi noble estatura
se enlace
con una sencilla esclava, ¡¡¡hrrmmpp!!!
Es cierto,
es una hembra
a todo dar . . .
pero no. Esta chatita patarajá
ya se está haciendo
demasiadas ilusiones, ¡¡¡hrrmmpp!!!

ELLA: Sí, amo y señor mío, tienes razón.
Ya lo sé que me quieres
y perdona mi necedad.

Es que nosotras
las mujeres
siempre soñamos con imposibles . . .

Y entre paréntesis Ella se dijo:

¡Huh! ¡Y para *eso* te di
mi sangre y mi pueblo!
Sí, ya lo veo, gringo desabrido,
tanto así me quieres
que me casarás
con tu subordinado Don Juan,
sin más ni más
como si fuera yo
un kilo de carne
—pos ni que fueras mi padre
pa' venderme a tu antojo
güero infeliz . . . ! ! !

Etcétera, etcétera.

La Malinche to Cortés and Vice Versa

(or, "Love Does Not Forgive, Not Even for Love")
1995

SHE: Give me your name, my lord and master,
so it shall adorn me. How I long
to carve it here, beside my own in the sand.
. . . because I am yours. Yours! and I want the
whole world to know about it.

HE: The whole world
knows about it already,
my dear Marina. You do not need
superfluous adornments.
I love you and that is enough.

And in parentheses HE says to himself:

Besides, hrrrmmmppp!!! It is unseemly
for a white man of *my*
noble standing to marry a
simple slave, hrrmmpp! . . . Although it's true,
as women go, she's a ten . . . but no.
This little barefoot social climber is letting
her ambitions run away with her, hrrmmpp!!!

SHE: Yes, O lord and master, you are *so* right.
I know full well that you love me, and
forgive my foolishness. It's that we silly
women always dream of things impossible . . .

And in parentheses SHE tells herself:

Huh! And for that I gave you
my blood and *my* people! O yes, I

see it now . . . you the white, the bland,
the utterly tasteless man
love me . . . you love me so much
that you plan to marry me off
to your subordinate Don Juan,
snap! like that! just as if I
were a pound of meat
—well, it's not as though you were *my* father
to sell me when and where you will,
my arrogant-cavalier-greedy-gringo friend . . . ! ! !

Etcetera, etcetera.

English translation by the author

Lesson in Semantics
1970

Men, she said,
   sometimes
      in order to
         say it

it is
   necessary
      to spit
         the word.

For Marsha
1983

> . . . *under the old sun*
> *we will know each other*
> *by the dust on our feet*
> —JOSÉ FLORES PEREGRINO

in the eye of my heart, I can see her:
the diligent artisan, committed
with clay & sand & water
designing, shaping, refining
the earthen cup, warm in her hands
—a drinking cup, the color of
soft midnight, a vessel of strength
     for daily wear

its pedestal is hollow
—always an achievement
in ceramics, and denoting
the need for space
     within space:
a freedom only autochthonal blood
     can fully understand

she wanted to give me something
that would speak in celebration
of her/our essence of
indigenous affinity:
               She, Choctaw
               I, Mexica

. . . Angela . . . here, take this cup
and whenever you drink of it
think of me . . .

dear Marsha! Marsha Gómez,
your gift will throb forever
within these words from my/our

RAZA LOVE   *RAZA NEED*   *RAZA EXPRESSION*

ésta noche, al llegarme
la onda de tu poesía
se abrió mi corazón
y te descubrí . . . hermana mía . . .

✎ Rosario Ferré

Conceptual Art
1992

It was hailing and bitter cold
and on the grate that blasts warm air
at the corner of Seventeenth
and Pennsylvania Avenue
three statues stood their ground
and stoically braved the elements.
They were burrowed in black burlap
sacks, with leper loincloths draped
over their heads in mud-packed
turbans, and from their spent
spattered cheeks you could tell
the whole world had already
driven past them. I never had
seen such a sight. The Mall
was thronged with holiday
strollers, who came and went
before the sleeping stone lions,
reveling in the gems of *Odyssey*,
the latest of the National Geographic's shows,
which focused on the heroism of Tibetan monks
who could go for thirty days
without food or drink,
and of Arab warriors who,
solidly ensconced on their trawling
camels, would never need a home,
but crisscrossed the Sahara
riding barefoot over burning

sands, all their worldly belongings
slung over their backs in dried-
out bladders. They hardly
looked at the sculpted trio
which stared off into space
like a crew of wide-eyed astronauts
just stepped off their ship,
doing their best to behave properly
and earn the right
to the Corcoran's doorstep.
No one wondered how far
they had come, or the curious
manner of their travels,
how long they had unwittingly
penanced, without Cokes
or even a hot dog, for the
inherent good of their souls,
how they had managed
to stake out their territory
from the swarm of other homeless
huddled together that windy morning
on the grates of less generous hells.
Perhaps they expected a vent
to be always a pin-up scenario
for touring Avedon vamps,
with moth-white skins
and Marilyn Monroe hair
skitting nervously over their skirts
as they lighted ablaze on dry ice;
or they figured it should be kept
as a stage for plaster sculptures
of the type George Segal casts
on the bodies of traveling vagabonds
so the warm air blasting upwards

will dry them out quickly,
or even as an altar for Louis Cifer himself
airing out his Paloma Picasso leather wings
after a tiresome voyage
on one of his flying cauldrons.
Nothing had prepared me for this,
the paramount indifference to the work,
to its hidden meaning,
the exquisite harmony of the composition,
as they rapidly walked by
turning their faces away just because
this was art of a different kind.

Positivo
1990

Errando por el camino de los siglos
de sueño en sueño avanzo y me detengo
a cada duda, a cada golpe y le confiero
la guerra a cada sombra que desmiente
a mi implacable corazón.
Sentado al fin del mundo
y apuntalada ya su vida en la mitad del día,
desespera de hallar lo que buscaba.
¡Oh indetenible corazón!
Unica raíz por la que subo
al fondo de mí misma y de esa furia
con la que sola mi alma se consuela, porque sola
me vio nacer;
revísteme a tu orden
convéxame a tu sueño
exhúmame a tu paciencia trashumante.
Por toda la ternura y todo el bien
que crece del amor y sus abismos;
por ese engaño fiel con que inventabas
la ilusión de no haber nacido solamente;
por el puro diamante y por la pura dicha
con que ocultas y rezumas tu saliva
a punto de estallar dentro del pecho;
por estarte endemoniado y ventilar
al borde de tu ventrículo derecho
la codicia de los degolladores,
de los que comen, tajan, pudren el amor
hincados sobre el cuello
del Dios;
por empeñarte en abrazar a tu esqueleto

por *llevarte un roble al labio,* porque amas;
por todas éstas cosas te prometo
que por éste mismo camino exigiré que pase
tu gemelo corazón impar.

Positive
1990

Wandering down time's passageways
from dream to dream I roam
from dream to blow,
bestowing contradiction upon every shadow
that strives to lie over my heart.
Seated at the end of the world
its beat propped up against the sky
it knows no rest in its unhappy quest.
Oh unyielding heart,
rare root by which I rise
to the depths of myself and of that wrath
which alone can soothe my soul, because alone
it stood, sole witness to my birth,
pair me under your cloak of arms,
couple me to your dreams,
exhume me to your unquiet peace!
In honor of all the tenderness and good
which grew from love's unfathomable abyss,
in honor of that faithful, soft-tongued fraud
with which you argued, in illusion, to mislead
by love's lone company,
in honor of that sheer diamond and that sheer luck
with which you hid and deceived
the bursting point of bliss within your chest,
because you dared bedevil and behest
at your left ventricle's edge
the executioner's greed
that would mince, slice, strike out the heart
while kneeling in prayer over the bowed neck
of the god,
because your skeleton persists in its embrace

because you *kissed an elm*, because you loved,
in honor of all these I swear my vow:
along this same, solitary road
your twin, uncoupled heart will one day
come to pass.

English translation by the author

Negativo
1990

Por la bondad con que le sirves a tu amado
un cafecito azul a cada hora;
por amamantar el miedo con que abrazas
en su abrazo todas las formas de la muerte;
por andar entre tacitas y legumbres
cuando tu amado despena hasta el tobillo
del mundo, cosechando y sembrando sus tesoros,
por los cantos del cisne y por la joya
que te obsequió en tu reciente plenilunio;
por amojamar tu corazón bajo la tierra
luego de sustraerlo a su costado;
por la sorda epifanía de tu humildad
y la amorosa estafa de tu falda;
por quedar siempre mudos en tu mano
los molinos de aceite y los del vino,
el número mayor o menor de tu ganado
y el humeante pulular de tus colmenas;
por nacer entre tu labio de hombre,
sobre tu lengua de hombre,
bajo tu hombro de hombre,
un corazón, que a golpes, más que hombre
un monte puesto encima rompería
en tanto que tus codos, tus piernas, y tus brazos
pálidos de aceite y hiel,
comprueban que eres mujer, y verdadera;
por moderarte, ser paciente y barajar
estándote contigo y con tu sombra;
por todas estas cosas y otras pocas

que al contemplar tu estado considero,
me pregunto quién eres, quién inventa
esta imagen que en mi espejo se detiene.

Negative
1990

Because you loved to serve your lover
a comforting blue coffee on the hour,
because you loved to nurse,
within the enclosure of his arm
a fear so great that it encompassed
all other forms of death,
because you minced daintily
amongst cups and saucers
while your lover tore down the world
razed to the stature of your ankle,
in honor of the swan song and the jewel
with which he wooed you on your last full-bellied moon,
for embalming your heart under the earth
after removing it from his rib,
in honor of your stone-dead birth
and the ever-loving swindle of your skirt,
in liege of those mills of oil and honey
which remained ever silent on your hand,
the lesser and the greater thronging of your flocks
and the swarming labyrinths of your hives,
for bearing, between your manly lips
upon your manly tongue
under your manly shoulder
a heart that, striking rudely, like a man's
would tear down a mountain by its fists
as your elbows, your legs, and your arms
melt in soft rivers of oil and bile
thus confirming the authenticity of your sex,
because you refrained wisely from excess, were prudent,
and as a young girl learned to shuffle,

dealing patiently twixt yourself and your shadow,
in honor of all these and a few others
which come to mind as I consider your condition
I wonder who you are, who might've imagined
this face that pauses by my mirror.

English translation by the author

ALICIA GALVÁN

Skin
1995

Have you ever noticed how
a snake sheds its skin?
We label him uncouth
to abandon so carelessly
that which was once
a part of him.

Devious, sly, lowly—
descriptive terms for
a creature crawling
on its belly.

We shed our skin, too,
or haven't you noticed?
Our cells slide off, disposed of daily,
though we're presumably superior
to these creatures
that make us cringe
with disgust.

Observe—however,
some humans
could pass for snakes.
At least the snake
doesn't wear
a disguise.

Penance?
1994

Sor Juana Inés de la Cruz,
philosopher, poet, nun, artist, dead at 46.
Cause of death: Premature retreat from the world by a human
callousness applied with a smooth misguided tongue.
A letter written in her cell and found 300 years later after
her death.

Upon choosing the monastic life to protect my intellect:

I walk long arched corridors that are dimly lit.
Reverent chants sung in low voice slip into my room through
the cracks in the wall.
My stiff white starched halo almost crushes my head.

In meditation, I see hands clasped discreetly
forming a prayer to stay or praying to escape.
No one knows.
In a litany of prayer we often cannot distinguish the words
formed softly tiptoeing,
ending in a hushed whisper.

Those shy glances that turn from me with downcast eyes,
is it humility or will they reveal anger in an unguarded
moment?

When I join the community in prayer,
are we all focusing on supreme spirituality
or just afraid to be out in humanity?

Hush! I hear the world breaking down the door
of my sanctuary.
Is nothing sacred in this sacred place?

❧ VICTORIA GARCÍA-GALAVIZ

Frida in the Nude
1993

Frida la pendeja
No, hardly so

I laughed
at the foolish actress,
hechando mentiras
de una vain
submissive Frida
y pintándose
dark connected eyebrows,
perdida en el espejo

Now Frida,
exposed to me

Her eyebrows
connect like
   her and Diego
   her and her roots
   her and the Earth

I can no longer
laugh

at this beautiful Mexicana,
con sus anillos de plata,
those my grandmother wore

her spirited strength,
that of a corazón

her orgullo,
that of nuestra raza

her womanhood,
which becomes me

La Gran Frida!

This she wears well

Malintzín . . . Marina
1994

Trying to tease
the idea
of survival,
a cobalt woman
born of waters
feels her feet
now scaleless
as burning sands
peel at each slither
of the path,
her tongue
once of rivers
turns to prickly pear
thick and gagging,
desperately
she grabs a green
outstretched limb,
only to pierce
her palm
on the tip of a maguey,
now bloody,
a sign, this life
now a whisper
will mute
and his,
the serpent Sun's
smothering tiger eyes
dictate
a new voice

✎ ALICIA GASPAR DE ALBA

La Frontera
1981

La frontera lies
wide open, sleeping beauty.
Her waist bends like the river
bank around a flagpole.
Her scent tangles in the arms
of the mesquite. Her legs
sink in the mud
of two countries, both
sides leaking sangre
y sueños.
      I come here
mystified by the sleek Río Grande
and its ripples and the moonlit curves
of tumbleweeds, the silent lloronas,
the children they lose.
In that body of dreams,
the Mexicans swim for years,
their fine skins too tight to breathe.
Yo también me he acostado con ella,
crossed that cold bed, wading
toward a hunched coyote.

Domingo Means Scrubbing
1982

our knees for Church.
'Amá splicing our trenzas tight
with ribbons, stretching
our eyes into slits. Grandpa
wearing his teeth.

Domingo means one of our tíos
passing out quarters
for the man with the basket
and me putting mine under
my tongue like the host.

Then menudo and Nina's
raisin tamales for dessert.
Our tías exchange Pepito
jokes in the kitchen
while we sneak a beer
into the bathroom,
believing the taste
will make our chi-chis grow.

Domingo means playing
a la familia with all our cousins,
me being the dad 'cause I'm
the oldest and the only one
who'll kiss the mom
under the willow tree.

After dark,
our grandmothers pisteando
tequila on the porch, scaring us

every little while: *La Llorona*
knows what you kids are doing!
'Amá coming out of the house
to drag the girls inside
pa' lavar los dishes.

Domingo means scrubbing.

Beggar on the Córdoba Bridge

(50 pesos for a poem)
1983

I want to keep you, old woman.
Knit your bones
in red wool, wear your eye
teeth around my neck—
amulets filled with sage.

You could teach me
the way of the gypsy:
how to dream
in an open field
(cotton or onion)
and let my hair grow long
roots in the mud.
How to take bread or fish
from the mouths of dogs,
travel bridges that are pure light,
tell the fortunes of rats.
From you, I could learn to read
the cracked, brown palm
of the Río Grande.

I want to keep you, old woman.
Weave your crow's feet
into my skin, polish
the black coins of your eyes—
currency of a higher kind.

❧ CELESTE GUZMÁN

La tía que nunca come azúcar
1996

I saved myself for your tío Rick.

My tía Alma blurts this out
over the sugar-free cake she bought me from HEB.

Today's my birthday,
so she talks about Tío Rick, who's dead.
Who's taken her small film of skin with him to the grave.
A worm ate it or a caterpillar or a roach sniffing at his collar.

I nibble the cake,
don't tell her of my tío's
summer stories on the back porch
about a place called Viet Nam and all the mujercitas:
una blondie que tuvo un tattoo of a stallion
                                    in the ridge of her back,

la filipina birthmarked with a print of a fist
                                    between her breasts,
y la alemana con una scar from the top of
            . her right shoulder to the bottom of her left pit.

With each gulp of milk
I swallow every body of every woman
my tío had ever slept with,
except my tía's.

Tío Rick, nomás would reirse
if you mentioned Alma. Ay, *tu tía.*

My tía, who lets me fall asleep
on top of her pudgy knees, my makeshift pillow;
ashes in my lashes from her cigarette and
the porcupine hair from her knees scratching my cheek.

Nopalita, my tío called her when she didn't shave.
She never laughed, just brushed my hair off my face.

When Tío Rick hit his head and did not wake up,
she was halfway through with a sugar donut.
She has stopped eating sugar since. *Para mi blood pressure.*
Pero nosotras sabemos the sweet reminds her
lips of his pan-dulcito tongue after café at night.

What does your back look like, are your
breasts the same size, do you like to be
tickled, are your thighs rough or soft up
there? Where did he take you that night?
Did he hold your back? Did your legs
scratch his cheeks?
My tía, que nunca come azúcar,
who will die
never having the taste of another man pass over her lips.

La cama de esperanza
1995

I sleep in my grandparents' bed
too large for one,
not wide enough for two;

dented
with the weight of twenty years of use,
splashed
with licks of café con leche and
soaked
with the sweat of sleep on sticky San Antonio nights.

From her cotton cavern,
Grandma spat mucus, blood, and
curses at the cancer as it ate her insides;

slit her eyes to the ceiling,
listened
to the bruja's last rites,

the screams and wails of the gitanos and
the murmuring and mumbling of the priest
dressed in black.

Grandpa laid next to her,
hand over his eyes,
choosing the dark comfort of blindness.

My first nightmare happened lying on his side,
a moth eating my pinky.
At seven, I fell off her edge and broke my arm.

Tonight, I settle myself on the ridge between
the imprints of their bodies.
My legs cross at themselves,

only buttocks balancing my weight; then
I roll and roll
spreading the fuzz under the mattress.

Then wait by the headboard
for the bed to break,
split a scream out of wood and bedsprings;

some awakening;
a twitching of foot,
a trembling of lash or

a simple belch from
deep
within my belly.

Coatlícue
1991

Days after atomic bomb days drop
and so I seek knowledge of the modern unknown
through the ancient ways.
Counsel me, Coatlícue,
she of the serpent skirt,
with a necklace of hands and hearts.
Oh Mother-Father
Goddess-God
Oh Universal Duality
where do we fit into your Aztec cosmology?

"1 sun 2 sun 3 sun 5
and everything shakes
mute or live
El Quinto Sol
The Fifth Sun
with earth's movement
we go down."

Yet we are fragments
of a planet already in pieces . . .
What say You, He-She, They
Coatlícue?

"I say same as have said
and will say again.

Dance
across the black ribboning earth.
this bloodless sun
in rage
is almost done."

Notes on Why Misogyny Is an Art Form
1994

Isn't it marvelous to be martyred?
Especially daily?
Although his infantile urge to
cut his teeth on your bones to the marrow
bites right through.

And although
in feeding him
he inevitably
grows stronger and moves on.

That is,
until his next need,
which, for him, necessarily exists
(that insecure instant
when his red blood runs anemic).

It's then that he will piecemeal
those bits of your bones together
and build you more beautifully
than ever before.

The Burning God
1991

Solamente contigo
my naked flesh melts away
y me siento bien. Together we'll
burn the purest flame. Oh embrace me again
—brazos y brazos para más abrazos—
to love another or another is the same.

Every time, como que me
estoy muriendo, hair hanging to the
floor, you hold me so gently and
enclose me with life. Yet, una palabra
de tus labios sagrados, and I shall fly
that is my vow, como la paloma blanca.

❧ MAYA ISLAS

Viaje de una mujer sola
1996

Detrás de la luz
una mujer camina,
abre la tierra
y la acaricia
porque no quiere equivocarse
de la ruta,
y huele las piedras
como si fueran rosas,
abraza a los muertos
como si estuvieran vivos . . .

La mujer se celebra
y enciende una vela a sus cabellos;
la oración le sale y la recorre
en una procesión de hormigas
que llevan el pan
para una cueva
donde se ama y se come
con la misma fuerza del espíritu.

Mientras escribo,
sigo un túnel
donde la mujer me espera
pare quemarme la ropa
en un instante de verdad.

Ya desnuda,
desciendo al mundo de los que oyen,
me quito la pasión,
los zapatos de tierra;
el poema me espera extendido en el mar,
como yo:
busca un país sin encontrarlo.

La mujer y su traje de luz
nos recibe en su cuerpo imaginario.
En su vientre
crecemos como dos flores intensas,
dos estados de mente . . . dos retratos.

One Woman's Journey
1996

Behind the light
a woman follows;
she opens the earth,
caresses it,
because she does not want
to miss the route;
she smells the stones
as if they were roses,
and embraces the dead
as if they were alive.

The woman celebrates herself
and lights a candle in her hair;
a prayer overflows from her body
and moves across her flesh
like a procession of ants
carrying bread to a cave
where loving and eating are done
with the same force of the spirit.

As I write,
I follow a tunnel
where the woman who is expecting me,
is ready to burn my clothes
with an instance of truth.

In nakedness,
I descend to the world
of the ones who listen;
I divest myself of passion
taking off my earthen shoes;

extended across the sea,
the poem awaits me
like me, it searches for a country
that cannot be found.

The woman in her garment of light
receives me with her imaginary body.
In her womb,
we grow like two intense flowers,
two states of mind,
two portraits.

English translation by the author

MARÍA LIMÓN

cuando se habla de nombres
1996

I

Cristóbal
he said to his bride-to-be
my name is Cristóbal
not lying really

Cristóbal the explorer
charting the continent divided
then bandaged with two puentes
marking the course
in a language his children
could not decipher
on a bicycle
meant more for Sunday outings
than for carrying
los bultos de sus sueños

Cristóbal who could not stand
who he was assigned to be
so he invented himself
only it didn't
take

Santiago
they told her
just before the priest pronounced her
his property

his name is Santiago
ditchdigger
albañil
enjarrador de mercados y teatros
the carrier of bags of bones
and poetry books
trapped under bid-sheet clipboards

II
Manuela
she said
my name is Manuela
never lying
much less about happiness

guinea pig
Manuela
who left lung fibers
on petri dishes
laid prayers
marked to nausea's rhythm
along hospital corridors
and learned English
only to survive

proud that
she and Santiago
went to the movies twice
danced only at weddings
and that she married
por vida

Manuela
her name only a few letters

removed from Emanuelle
happy to serve godchildren
and the country of believers
she'd call a congregation
if it were allowed

III
María del Socorro Limón Castro
they sighed
last of the girl children
the tail end of
María de los Dolores
and
María de los Angeles
good girl
overfed the rich greasy
hope
saved for the children born
on the Texas side of the puddle
now confused with a great river

wealth and happiness
was hers they knew
could feel it in her bones
broken but a few times
damage not enough
to cripple

lesbiana-chicana
más-india-que-la-chingada
with-an-attitude
she says
more shield
than name

maríalimón
some say
not knowing that
any combination of letters
is insufficient to cover
the expanse

❧ RITA MAGDALENO

Night Flight
1996

Witch or *bitch*, I've been referred to
as both. Still, you've never seen
the wings I grow at night.
They are luminous. I am
the hummingbird spinning
emerald light and my heart
beats crimson. Tonight, I
am full of sweet juice.

Other times you have named me
harshly—*puta, whore, piece
of ass*. But I will tell you this:
Once I was the black flower
you tried to pluck; I was the Spanish
girl you raped; I was the dancer
you tangoed with in a Chicago bar;
I was the waitress you undressed
with your eyes; I was the midwife
who received you; I was the silver
snake in your dreams.

The nest is empty now, the magic
bundle strapped to my back. Tonight
I will fly a straight, clear route across
the moon, across the dreaming
border, across el río, no stopovers
for me, tonight.

Wake up; open your window.
Perhaps you will see
the magic direction
where women go
at night.

The Leaving
1996

Everywhere, the fragile smell
of rain. And despite the fact
that we were optimistic
about our future, the European
river still pulled me away

like *Llorona*. Then I
dressed in white, drank
only black coffee, took
a dark lover. Slowly I began
to understand the variously

sensitive scars in my memory.
And when a dark ship arrived,
I entered that water. Finally I
understood the possibility
of finding the way home.

There, I imagined the child
I loved waiting patiently
at the table, her small
hands opening
to receive bread
and milk.

DEMETRIA MARTÍNEZ

To Keep Back the Cold
1986

1.
Squares of plastic tacked
to window frames
like fog cut to size,
huddling about our house winter long.
Hooks in walls for coats and hats,
logs stacked in the stairwell,
rags we stuff at the foot of the door.
The porch leans on its beams
like a cat braced to pounce
at the first snow swirl.

Drafts enter everywhere,
through sinkholes, floorboards.
Frost salts outlets,
night cracks and floats south
leaving kernels of ice
in every orifice.
We sprinkle kindling with kerosene,
flick the match,
flames from the mouth
of the hearth
light the path to bed,
we speak in our sleep
of keeping away the cold.

2.

Morning mounts the tents
in a refugee camp,
women stir fires with sticks,
feeding flames with whatever
their children cannot eat.
Breath claws out of sunken mouths,
a brown hand points to the sun
as if to ease the body's chill.
A woman cups her eyes,
turns from the camera,
tries to remember
the color green
as she walks this pinched
rind of earth,
a city of carps
so starved
first winds will collapse it.

3.

In a house where 80-degree air
is delivered at the side entry,
where drapes fill up like lungs
and hold back the winds,
even here drafts leak
from mirrors, aquariums,
from pockets of woolen pants.

Parents and children tuck heads
in prayer then carve steaks
but by sunset a blizzard
balls furiously above
the oak table,

faces untraceable.
The children shatter like bulbs,
shards scuttle over carpets,
an explosion of such force
tolerates no bare flesh,
parents in goggles and boots
pick glass splinters
off the floor,
tongues frozen
to the roofs of mouths.

4.

It will take more than Einstein
to warm such a day,
and should the Salvation Army
really take over we will need more
than soup to start the thaw.
Old tricks are spent.
Like a war veteran in a wheelchair
who reads that running cures indifference,
we rip magazines
ram them between logs.
What are we to do?
Unwilling inventors in an Ice Age,
ready to burn pews.

5.

Kneel before this hearth,
listen to bark crack in the grate
as flames peak like petals.
To whom do we pray?
Against whom do we revolt
for such sorrows as a baby
frozen in a manger?

I will not sing of it,
I will not sing.
Feel ashes storm into your eyes,
you will burn
with questions of continents,
you will turn and ache
all night forever, longing
to keep back the cold.

Nativity: For Two Salvadoran Women, 1986–1987

1987

Your eyes, large as Canada, welcome
this stranger.
We meet in a Juárez train station
where you sat hours,
your offspring blooming in you
like cactus fruit,
dresses stained where breasts leak,
panties in purses tagged
"Hecho en El Salvador,"
your belts, like equators,
mark north from south,
borders I cannot cross,
for I am a North American reporter,
pen and notebook, the tools
of my tribe, distance us
though in any other era I might
press a stethoscope to your wombs,
hear the symphony of the unborn,
finger forth infants to light,
wipe afterbirth, cut cords.

"It is impossible to raise a child
in that country."

Sisters, I am no saint. Just a woman
who happens to be a reporter,
a reporter who happens
to be a woman,
squat in a forest, peeing
on pine needles,

watching you vomit morning sickness,
a sickness infinite as the war in El Salvador,
a sickness my pen and notebook will not ease,
tell me, ¿Por qué están aquí?,
how did you cross over?
In my country we sing of a baby in a manger,
finance death squads,
how to write of this shame,
of the children you chose to save?

"It is impossible to raise a child
in that country."

A North American reporter,
I smile, you tell me you are due
in December, we nod,
knowing what women know,
I shut my notebook,
watch your car rock
through the Gila,
a canoe hangs over the windshield
like the beak of an eagle,
babies turn in your wombs,
summoned to Belén to be born.

La Buena Pastora: The Good Shepherdess
1996

This is a thirsty land:
In the land is a valley,
In the valley is a path,
In the path is a lamb,
In the lamb is a longing,
In the longing is a pool,
In the pool is an eye,
In the eye is a hope,
In the hope is a woman,
In the woman is a prayer,
     A prayer moist with rain.
Rain in the prayer,
Prayer in the woman,
Woman in the hope,
Hope in the eye,
Eye in the pool,
Pool in the longing,
Longing in the parched lamb,
Lamb in the path,
Path in the valley,
Valley in the land,
     This is the thirsty land.

Sonrisas
1985

I live in a doorway
between two rooms. I hear
quiet clicks, cups of black
coffee, *click, click* like facts
   budgets, tenure, curriculum,
from careful women in crisp beige
suits, quick beige smiles
that seldom sneak into their eyes.

I peek
in the other room señoras
in faded dresses stir sweet
milk coffee, laughter whirls
with steam from fresh *tamales*
sh, sh, mucho ruido,
they scold one another,
press their lips, trap smiles
in their dark, Mexican eyes.

Bilingual Christmas

Do you hear what I hear?
1985

Buenos días and *hasta luego*
in boardrooms and strategy sessions.
Where are your grateful holiday smiles,
bilinguals? I've given you a voice,
let you in
to hear old friends tell old jokes.
Stop flinching. Drink eggnog. Hum along.

> Not carols we hear
> whimpering
> children too cold
> to sing
> on Christmas eve.

Do you see what I see

adding a dash of color
to conferences and corporate parties
one per panel or office
slight south-of-the-border seasoning
feliz navidad and *próspero año nuevo*, right?
Relax. Eat rum balls. Watch the snow.

> Not twinkling lights
> we see but
> searchlights
> seeking illegal aliens
> outside our thick windows.

Curandera
1984

They think she lives alone
on the edge of town in a two-room house
where she moved when her husband died
at thirty-five of a gunshot wound
in the bed of another woman. The *curandera*
and house have aged together to the rhythm
of the desert.

She wakes early, lights candles before
her sacred statues, brews tea of *yerbabuena*.
She moves down her porch steps, rubs
cool morning sand into her hands, into her arms.
Like a large black bird, she feeds on
the desert, gathering herbs for her basket.

Her days are slow, days of grinding
dried snake into powder, of crushing
wild bees to mix with white wine.
And the townspeople come, hoping
to be touched by her ointments,
her hands, her prayers, her eyes.
She listens to their stories, and she listens
to the desert, always, to the desert.

By sunset she is tired. The wind
strokes the strands of long gray hair,
the smell of drying plants drifts
into her blood, the sun seeps
into her bones. She dozes
on her back porch. Rocking, rocking.

At night she cooks chopped cactus
and brews more tea. She brushes a layer
of sand from her bed, sand which covers
the table, stove, floor. She blows
the statues clean, the candles out.
Before sleeping, she listens to the message
of the owl and the *coyote*. She closes her eyes
and breathes with the mice and snakes
and wind.

La Migra

1994

1

Let's play La Migra.
I'll be the Border Patrol.
You be the Mexican maid.
I get the badge and sunglasses.
You can hide and run,
but you can't get away
because I have a jeep.
I can take you wherever
I want, but don't ask
questions because
I don't speak Spanish.
I can touch you wherever
I want but don't complain
too much because I've got
boots and kick—if I have to,
and I have handcuffs.
Oh, and a gun.
Get ready, get set, run.

2

Let's play La Migra.
You be the Border Patrol.
I'll be the Mexican woman.
Your jeep has a flat,
and you have been spotted
by the sun.
All you have is heavy: hat,
glasses, badge, shoes, gun.
I know this desert,
where to rest,

where to drink.
Oh, I am not alone.
You hear us singing
and laughing with the wind,
Agua dulce brota aquí, aquí, aquí,
but since you can't speak Spanish,
you do not understand.
Get ready.

✒ ELVIA PADILLA

The border, she is a woman
1995

barricaded and defended by bodies
she is scooped up in a bucket
boiled and drunk down
she is a raging trap
her waters hot with death's stink
a playa in the summer
La Mexican Beach!

a brewing soup of rubber tires, soda cans,
and desert weeds
a baptismal, a public bath
a muddy birth canal
forging a doubled people
who leap and dance from her laughing mouth

a deep mark through the solid earth
accentuating a *difference*. Still,
she personifies the whole—
the whole
a twisted, simmering road
an incessant, turbulent flow

Woman as a River
1995

I am floating and pale
in the wave of his body
silent, waiting
I just jumped in

all I can feel
is his damp skin
the ocean that is his mouth
the curve from neck to shoulder
I would have stayed there forever
a woman turned river

with no source
and no destination
just a river
nothing living in the silt
nor on the sandy floor

nothing swimming
between the restless currents
and no bridges across it

Leave Her for Me
1995

Do you comb her sleepy hair with your brown fingers?
Is she not afraid to live through your whims as I am?

Does she even speak our language, tightened tongues exploring
every slick and sharp curve of mouth?
Can her body weave around you like a lovesick serpent?
Will she lead you to sleep with her humming and caressing,
a deep sleep safe and without morning?

I am the one who would drown in a dirty river for you
Abandon my past and all else just to get to the other side
Force my body through chain-link fence
Lose my fortune to hounds of night
Cross by train in a boxcar sealed tight . . . *for you*
What would she do?

⮞ ANABELLA PAIZ

Moon Phases
1995

1.   First
A young girl wrapped in damask
her cool virginity a shawl
fenced inside her space
by the sharp points of the stars.
Perching on limbs of dark branches
the nubile siren waits
to unfold and no longer be
candlelight to the sun.

II.   Full
Unveiled and shining,
she roams the sculpture garden
followed by her mantle's train.
Mistress of a divided mansion
she does as she pleases
when the sun is away:
extends her field of gravity
orders fluids to rise
collects seeds
orchestrates lovers' sighs.
Her light spills on golden pillows
as she dreams of bringing down the wall.

III.   Last
She has heard she'll be most wanted
if she makes herself scarce

shows one leg, winks one eye
dims her face behind a shade of hair.
She likes to eat with her fingers
rendezvous under a hooded arch
wants to be a seraphic caprice
scintillating prima donna
in a circle of stars
but the Little Dipper calls her
the Great Teaser;
she is afraid the name has caught.

IV.   New
Shrouded in dark veils
burning incense
the ebony priestess prays
over craters and ridges.
She walks barefoot on brambles
howls like a mad woman
wears a mask
waiting for her cloistering to end.

❧ Deborah Parédez

A Cartography of Passions
1996

i.
here: our forsaken home

mesa breaks desert
dialing curve of mountain

territory of anthropology
of the outlaw

where you taught me how to shoot that .22 real good
rifle butt steadied against the shoulder socket

a wild pulsing third arm

postures of stillness and reserve
practiced cunning of the predator

in the end   shattered
bottles among cowering piñones

here: the natives have never been safe

ii.
curious sentimental boy intent
on the romance of expedition

clever cynical woman intent
on the Romantic trope

mi cielo mi mar mi luna mi tierra
language of Spanish occupation

diligent engineers
we divide and enter

mapping for future travels

the sheets marked, desk cluttered:
pencil shavings graphs incomplete stanzas

metaphors and equations
of isolated fixed points

like Malinches we are left
harboring the remains of one

another's labor

iii.
la migra   your mind

skilled at expulsion
vigilant surveillance

those refused entry interest me
those forced to settle elsewhere

ours is an patrolled encounter
my mind is what interests you

creases of cerebrum   electric
streams coursing through these fissures

a landscape ripe for excavation

you are brother to Isabella
in devices and commands

always the agenda
the missionary plans

and like the others
you will insist on exile

and I am no Circe

no magical powers
no victim of narrative

just a woman with these few words
a woman who has peered through the barrel of a loaded gun

leaving nothing intact

Converging Boundary

para "las girlfriends"
1993–97

Sí, mujeres, sí, sabemos, we know all about boundaries
we inhabit them, reside in these mountains
between two cultures converging, massive plates
of earth colliding earth colliding earth colliding,
neither willing to subduct, to submit. Here
at this range of cooled magma, we are locked,
bound to the rocks.

Daily the eagles swoop, talons intent on blinding
us, the ones who gave away the family secrets
the stories guarded like fire. Our translations
printed in English, language of los gringos.
But we know there are those who would seize
these stories, our confessions, for their own uses.
They descend on us, descend as preying birds.
So we are clever, disguise ourselves under metaphors,
allusions, careful languages: shields against these beasts.
We work diligently, rub the sticks together
the smoke ascending, occluding their flight path,
curls of smoke, escritura ellos no pueden descifrar.

☙ TERESINKA PEREIRA

Alabanza al gusano
1996

Los gusanos son nuestra
esperanza de ser útiles
por la última vez:
nos limpian de la inmundicia
terrena y nos reciclan.

Hay que darles las gracias
a los hermanos gusanos,
que nos transforman
de carne podrida
en árbol, flor o pájaro.

Hay que darles las gracias
por comernos la hedionda piel
y metamorfosearla en fragante
parte de un hermoso paisaje.

¡Yo los quiero, hermanos gusanos!
Y también amo a todas las criaturas
mortuarias: hormigas, grillos,
larvas, parásitos, luciérnagas,
moscas y cochinillas.

Hoy día les doy anticipadamente
las gracias por regresarme
a la fragancia de mi piel,
a mis vuelos locos, mis ilusiones,
y mis perpetuas tristezas . . .

Poem to Praise Worms
1996

Worms are our hope
to be useful
for the last time:

They clean us from
our earthly filthy flesh
and recycle it into a
tree, flower, or bird.

We should thank them
for eating our rotten skin
to a metamorphic fragrant
part of a beautiful landscape.

I love you, brother worm!
And I love all of you
busy mortuary creatures:
ants, crickets, larvae,
parasites, fireflies, insects:

I thank you beforehand
for taking my skin back to
its original fragrance,
to its dream flights,
wonders, and perpetual sadness . . .

English translation by the author

On Seeing Vermeer's Geographer
1996

I.

Nieuw Amsterdam. And here? Terra incognita. A mere 35 degrees. Not far. A whale's leap, a way stop on the winged flyway. Here to There: Land Known to Land Without a Name. Formless. Incognita. And yet as the crow flies, not far. Sailing from here to there: a half year. Half a year of a man's life, perhaps. Or a woman's—if she chooses.

II.

I see them from my window, through the mullioned lozenges, ready to embark, white caps unfurled like the wings of lofting shore birds, good citizens of Delft. Substantial. Potato people. Householders clustering amid their sacks, their bursting sea chests. Bound for a world at the edge of seas, 180 degrees here on the Mercator. A stretch of compass leg, the mere spread of an angle. Insignificant. And yet. And yet.

III.

They call me geographer. Of what? I ask myself. Of parchment. Of these white scrolls. Tunnels, call them. Tunnels of light. Cloistered here. Caught amid my quills and ink pots. Locks in place, robe tightly cinctured. Linen freshly laundered. Crimped. Impeccable. Impeccable as my measurings. 180 degrees longitude. 45 degrees latitude from the cincture of the earth.

IV.

And they? Bound for? Equatorial waters, the Antilles, perhaps. Nieuw Amsterdam. Solid citizens. Solidly rooted, their stout

Dutch legs cased in stockings knit of unbleached wool, histories of winter hearth fires, long winter nights preparing. A half year. Half a year at best.

V.

And I? Come March, this room will claim me. Claim me still. As it must always claim me. My scrolls of parchment, my compass and my sextants. Recording my findings. Issuing new maps of lands already named. Drawing. Tracing littorals, populating distant seas: here a griffin, there a mermaid, the slathering sea serpent. Whalers lost in the Cape of Storms. The seas shifty-eyed and scheming, crest and trough. Restless. Watching for the foundering vessel, ready to swallow the venturing sailor in its maw.

And I Safe. Here. Stopped as Vermeer painted me. Tunneled in white light.

The original Pineda to immigrate to this continent in 1521 was a cartographer.

Blue Madonna
1976

My blue madonna of the thousand faces
is nodding, smacked-out, her skin neon blue
like the rocks in a geological exhibit
lit with the fluorescent light
of a thousand crab claws
in the bloodstream.

Her black hair bound in the tiara of Shiva,
her blue skin a Kathakali of the dead,
the deep black brows still, still in a sleep
deader than death, my blue madonna is
posing for us: artist as corpse, she is stiller
than stone. Death, stone, she outdoes them:
her death itself breathes.

⮝ Pina Pipino

White Scarves
1995

30,000 disappeared in ten years.
Their mothers still circle Plaza de Mayo,
in Buenos Aires,
go round and round every Thursday,
looking for traces—
perhaps a lock of hair?
the costly black sandals?
the unfinished thesis?
the blue skirt with white stripes?
the first book of poems?
the old sweater?
the newlywed gold band?
the student card?
the jacket with a missing button?
the toy truck with a broken wheel?
the red tie with tiny white dots?
the rattle with a pink ribbon?
the monogrammed silk shirt?
the ripped jeans?
the pacifier?
Heads covered in white scarves
like beacons of light
illuminating their path,
mothers trail their immortal quest.
I could have been one of them
had I stayed behind,
had my children written poems,

had they befriended poets,
had they worked for a newspaper,
had they defended the poor,
had they protested for a raise,
had they been rebellious students,
had they loved a rebellious student,
had they been there.

Aliens
1994

Living in Essex Fells, New Jersey,
was like living in a park,
surrounded by dogwood trees,
pines, oaks, and magnolias,
terse lawns of well-cared grasses,
sinuous, impeccably clean lanes
and quiet.
We were known as the "aliens,"
the word "immigrant"
was outdated by then.
I learned that to qualify
as immigrants we would
have had to come a hundred
years earlier,
when Irish, Polish, Italian,
and other immigrants arrived
at Ellis Island
to be processed and accepted
into this land of plenty.
When I saw the motion picture
Aliens, I definitely knew
that I was not an alien,
like that evil being
bent on destroying its host.
And I told my children,
"We are immigrants
—whether the folks in Essex Fells
like it or not."

❧ NICOLE POLLENTIER

Keeper of the Word
1993

fingertip the matter
(touch it with careful birdlike wonder)

    imagine now
imagine a little girl whole
    maybe that godhead was blind
imagine that little girl
    maybe that buddha went crazy
blown to a million pieces
    what if that jesus did have dirty hands?
fall into sleep

    and she's woken up to find
    a tree naked in the doorway

she's crashed (head) on with a naked tree
planted firmly in the road
    she
           has
           been
                  detoured
from the path
directed in
                  the side streets
where all the cars are phantom
and every navigation

points to deeper internal wounds
    (soft spots on an apple)

ripped green from a branch
she surely
should rot

    the dream:
all the people are suddenly naked

                (shock of bare flesh
                an edge like a papercut)

they shed their clothes
as if secrets were made to be told
run for the water
are blessed and born

                again and again

if only words could be
so simple
just take off

                what those dirty hands said

all the dead leaves
chop down that infernal tree

                she tries but in his eyes

there are thick
roots

note the power of the word
somehow stronger than the punctures
of birds who invade branches

       (when the beak is gone
       those dirty kisses will fade)

this poem is a history of the etchings
of angry mouths
not flat as photos
the poem goes past the color print
the shadowy negative
even the action itself

       white flash
       dead in time

the poem
is the keeper of the word

       (I) am only a map

always fishing
kodiak, alaska
1996

> "he is so beautiful and
> sometimes I am so
> overcome by him
> that I touch his side
> with just the tips
> of my fingers as if
> he were a shiny salmon"
> —SEPTEMBER PASSED

the fireweed twisted
all those fish dying
dead or partially decayed
october
sergeant creek
a stream of conscious corpses
and washed-up skeletons in the rain
his reign of days
I patrolled the shore
looking for a complete set of bones
my graveyard expanded
he thought of new rules
red salmon don't eat
open-mouthed for what purpose
that useless row of teeth
down
the bellies dropped
no one could've hoped to lay
no need for those eggs
but we were always fishing
crossing lines

❧ BEATRIZ RIVERA

Lament of the Terrorist
1996

Florida swamp filled with crushed seashells, it sparkles
It was meant to be a field of houses for sale
Straight line of Jacks in the Box popping up, next ten!
New land yielded hollow fruit and empty crab shells
For hermit families, another ten! claim yours
A tiny down payment feel sorry for money
Four numbers were tattooed on each stucco facade
That's how you could tell yours apart from the others
Besides painting the door a bright different color

It was an unsafe house, malignity, green-grooved
And grey two-edged sharp coral path made your feet bleed
Your blood oozed into the hot earth like the fifties
Into the sixties, unsafe house, Mad Queen of Clubs
The backyard, a ribbon of grass fringing a screen
Warped and billowy, keeping a pool free of leaves

But there were no trees!
Ay! Ay! Ay!

A war waif, she's no Queen of Hearts
Female terrorist, specialist
Genius in the art of warfare
Night stick, morning star, pistola
Floozy, name it, she's number one

Ay! Ay! Ay!

Whichever way she looks, left! right!
It's chlorine blue and cement white

Oh! The pain is white!

Quick! Give it an address
Late Saturday Night Special
A dumb dumb graphic address
Azimuthal projection
Where to drop the dirty bomb
Cardinal letters, numbers
No names, a freedom address
Truly impersonalized

Oh! It hurts like mad!

The dull pain summons
Queen of Clubs, it's time!

Sawed-off shotgun
Tear-gas grenade
Automatic
Escopeta
Ready for this
Better past? fire!

Leave a Hansel and Gretel trail
Of quick flammables, turpentine
Gasoline, resentment, Cognac
Jingo, bimbo, jinx, light a match!

Hear the Deep Song! Ay!

Echo of a vain prayer
Terror be propitious

End it once and for all
The beast's everlasting
Mercury and diamond

      Day of pain and panic
      Hear the deep song, ay!

The cycle that ebbs and flows
Dies and takes on other forms
Put all your damn explosives
In the same wicker mailbox
The place where something went wrong
Identical houses, rows!

      Just like everyone else, oh no!

Jumped and almost drowned
Killed an animal
Messy place, the root
Of all the badness

      The pain is back!

From the eternal summer
Of sadness, of violence

In the pool forevermore
Fingers wrinkled like Niobe's
Showed their true colors
Death white
What they really are
Death white

Hear the deep song, it sobs
It says nothing at all
Like a suicide note

✎ Eliana Suárez Rivero

Three for Two
1978

i — I should have danced all night instead of talking nonsense

    in the beginning
    there was the WORD:
    I can laugh now
    to think how full it sounded
    mixed with the music
    and how it made
    my very own little nails
                tremble
    so I spilled a glass of beer
    and smiled at his open red face,
    mentally growing tall
                under the light
    in the end
    there was only one word:
    we have come a long way
    but it's back to basic me,
              baby

ii — What now, our very own (Western) union?
    the message that man never sent
    but I, a woman, received loud and clear
    read like this:
                "I regret to inform you
    that I am dropping your name
    from my mailing list   COMMA

dropping your face
from my memory   COMMA
and in general

                    dropping
                        YOU
because I have determined
that you are dangerous
to my independence

and to my much-beloved freedom
                            STOP

iii — so what if the whole world forgets about me?
I still have my books
and I know how to walk in the rain
                        (when there is any)
and I can teach others how to read
            poems that are too long
and I can make an omelette
and wear my sadness
                under a wide-brimmed hat
and paint my lips with purple
and speak with a loud voice
                    to help my sisters
and most of all
—oh yes—
            I can say that I hate his guts
carefully putting my tongue
                inside my cheek

History Revisited: In Québec, with a Friend
1979

🐚 *Jacques de Sores, a French filibuster,*
captured the port of Havana, Cuba, in
the sixteenth century.

Jacques
surrounded my green island
four centuries ago.
He was the most determined pirate
in the Caribbean:
French eyes, a taste for Indian women,
and the sweetest smile
under a galleon's sails.

But his body was a place of confusion:
a hollow wooden stomach,
two solid legs
filled with the rarest wine
that crossed the ocean,
and a black patch that crossed his chest
right over the left ventricle.
His heart
had more colors than a parrot:
it kept repeating,
"Jacques wants a lover,
Jacques wants a lover."
No soda crackers for this pirate!
Nobody could resist him:
least of all Indian maidens.

❧ CARMEN GIMÉNEZ ROSELLÓ

Frida
1995

Frida loves like all she can see is living under
umbrellas that unfold as big as skies.
Her aunt told her, "I'm the ancestor, mind me:

stand out under that shady elm there,
wait for the milkman, and pay our debt."
Frida did. Five years later another man,

dark, covered with the smell of smoke,
took her down in his car. Quarters plinking
on pool tables made more noise than she did.

He slipped up and left names and places. She
told him about the milkman, his hands
scraping the old elm's bark.

They left each other with the copper taste
of shame. This and others, she tells me. They
begin, they have middles, and they end.

I've got her story on a napkin.
See where she blots her lipstick?
While we're together we talk about pleasing

a man. "Not just spunk." She winks. "I've got notions."
Once Frida waited for her man wrapped in Xmas lights.
Once Frida spent a hundred dollars on a pair of red heels.

Is this bad? I've told her all the things
I've learned. What it is to be on your own. How
I can go to the movies alone but Frida laughs

like Frida laughs. Once tired of just watching
I pulled into a man like Frida does. He had boots
and a wide hat that he rested on a jerky knee.

We slept badly together in an apartment that smelled
of beer and the mold that grows on bread. He told me
he loved me. While he slept his woman left shaky messages

on his machine. The next day Frida stroked the places where
he had worn my skin thin. "You haven't got it in you,"
she promised. I try to remember the reasons

it's wrong. Maybe you have to be standing in a certain light
but I see Frida the way she burns truer than smoke.

Plaza de Armas, Lima
1996

I
Motor oil and urine do not mix in puddles
on the corner where the man sells whistles
that cry like an infant or crow like a cock.
I buy French soap from a girl dressed in layers of rough sack.
Her socks bunch into crowns at her ankles.

II
The old women enter the church
in the morning, heads bowed,
cheap lace mantillas at their throats.
Then they crowd on corners waiting
for microbuses. They smell like work
and candles and lavender. Their backs
are sometimes bent forward, always
wide as if at night they became tables.

III
A man paints caricatures at the corner
sitting on a stool at a cardboard easel
and renders wide-eyed figures
with the palace in the foreground.
A mother drags her children through a crowd
of shoppers. An old woman knits. At his feet
are the pastel sketches he makes
between guests. They are rose
and orange sunbursts over a faded palace.

IV
There is tragedy at some crests and at others
a breathless view of a city built on old gold

pounded into silt and a lake.

At night, I believe all cities to be populated by

ghosts in a splendid plumage.

Nothing broken except the rays of sun when they pass over them.

❧ BEVERLY SÁNCHEZ-PADILLA

Mali
1991

Just one more mestiza in contemporary United States
looking, longing, uncovering the
tangled history of
burned knots
to be
untied
to sleep at night.

MALINELLI,
MALINTZÍN,
MALINCHE,
DOÑA MARINA.

An identity problem is obvious.
Who was this woman who has been blamed
for opening up her Native people's legs
for all the Spanish warriors to enter . . .
500 years of punishment by some,
glorification by others.

Just one more mestiza,
molding the role model
Remythologizing,
Recapturing,
Rewriting,
Reinterpreting the story as per
the books that lie,

to each other
page to page
face-to-face.

Her father, a rich and powerful cacique,
died when she was very young.
Her mother married again, and
having a son,
conceived the infamous idea of securing
to this offspring
Marina's rightful inheritance.
    —WILLIAM H. PRESCOTT, *HISTORY OF THE CONQUEST OF MEXICO*

There goes the romantic notion
that natives at the time
were
at least somewhat matriarchal.
From noble princess
to slave
and back and forth (depending on where
you start herstory).
The denial of her mother,
for the love and lust of a new husband.
A kind of double doom.
Let's put that story on the back
burn her
of
misogyny.

Ah,
that is the woman
the silent beauty
Ever-suffering
Giving,

y giving,
y más giving.
A silver soldieress.
COULD IT BE NUESTRA SEÑORA HERSELF?

An Aztec woman? . . .
Think once more with your *informed* research.
Your gut
our moral memory.
MALINELLI, MALINALLI from PAINELLA
(born 1502?
died 1527?)
A NATIVE WOMAN *UNDER AZTEC RULE*
YES.
Who served as
Brilliant,
Passive
Lingual
Adviser
Translator to the
Outside Spanish war god
Cortés
1519.

A woman of savvy.
Street, slave savvy.
Who never liked the
bloodletting of Montezuma.
Never liked the lack of education for female natives.
Compulsory only for the males.

¿LLORONA?
¿NUESTRA SEÑORA?
No . . . nomás una de las huercas

Con ganas.
Con brains.
Una de las cucarachas
Que saben.

I BELIEVE she went up to Jerónimo de Aguilar before
Cortés came.
She learned some idioma español from this early shipwrecked man.
He learned Mayan as a prisoner.
The two of them
full will in hand
walked up into the Cortés ship AND
In a three-way translation
Nahuatl, Mayan, Spanish, and
back around again
spoke.
Did not communicate.
Just spoke.

With mangoes, wreaths of marigolds for the
four-legged gods who detached at the waist then reattached
for riding and killing.

Pués what did she have to lose?
Nada.
Nomás una sociedad con

PYRAMIDS
  THAT
    WERE
      SO
        HARD
          ON THE SLAVES TO BUILD

          SO HIGH ON THE SLAVES TO BUILD

Pués what did she have to lose?
A community with
much maguey letting,
blood betting.

Pués what did she have to gain?
A change of administration
where all the mujeres would go to school.
Montezuma, a wild polytheistic warrior ruler.
Cortés, a wild monotheistic warrior ruler.

Pués what did she have to lose?

Mallinelli
Who were you?
The victim Inés wants us to see? (And we do.)
The mother, our earth, Inés wants us to love? (And we have.)
The whore Octavio makes us live with? (And we are.)
The technocratic robot translator of the many, many sources?
The psychologically perverted woman who was abused
by her mother?

Yes . . . ¡y qué!

Or the ethereal horsewoman who is superior because
she is like a man:

Admira tan lúcida cabalgada
y espectáculo tal Doña Marina,
India noble al caudillo presentada,
de fortuna y belleza peregrina.
Con despejado espíritu y viveza
gira la vista en el concurso mudo;
rico manto de extrema sutileza

con chapas de oro autorizarla pudo,
prendido con bizarra gentileza
sobre los pechos en ayroso nudo;
reyna parece de la Indiana Zona
varonil y hermosísima Amazona.
　　　—William H. Prescott

MALINALLI
una de las mujeres mexicanas
who learned (too late) that Cortés and Monte were
the same.

MALINTZÍN
una de las mujeres chicanas
who believed that structural changes could happen.

MALINCHE
una de las mujeres indígenas
who was searching for
a
balance
of
powers within herself—CREATIVE,
　　　　　　　　EROTIC,
　　　　　　　　WARRIOR
　　　　　　　　MOTHER EARTH
　　(words of Ohki Semeni, Mohawk Medicine Woman)

DOÑA MARINA
una de las indias
con bastante fe

MALINELLI
una de las mujeres
who knew her power.

208

🐂 RAQUEL VALLE SENTÍES

Laredo

1989

¡Te odio! ¡Te amo!
Odio your dusty unpaved streets
and blistering days
of a never-ending summer.

Amo tus fiery sunsets
that tint *el cielo*
with burnished copper
streaked with peach and purple.

Odio the dry, parched *tierra*,
open cracks waiting for rain
like baby birds waiting for worms.

Amo the Depot District
con sus stately mansions,
decaying dowagers,
remnants of a bygone era.

Odio la cloaca the *Río Grande*
has become . . . thick, fetid, murky,
stench fouling the air
like the slop pails of long ago.

Amo the nearness of *México*,
divided by a border,
united by our *raíces*.

Odio el downtown,
what we have made of it,
an old harlot
whose beauty no amount of paint
can bring back.

Amo las myriad bougainvilleas.
purple, orange, red, white,
whose vivid colors
brighten *patios* all year round.

Odio los cadillos
that stick painfully to my bare feet
and the weeds that never die.

Amo your Tex-Mex culture
where *hablar español*
is an asset, not a liability.

Odio the spray-painted fences,
zombied messages of decadent youth.

Pero, more than anything, *Laredo*,
amo your people, *mi gente*,
a pesar de sus defectos,
por sus muchas cualidades,
que te aman y te odian como yo.

❧ CARMEN TAFOLLA

New Song
1978

lágrimas and loneliness
   and an open wound
     once more attacked

   and a distance doubled over on its own echo,
    a death buried into its own corpse.

I—a shawl of many colors
   woven from threads opposing
   neither fine wine nor adobe
   yet both
    and new music.

   Dances late into a spiraled night
    secret and shout-songed celebrations
    Wild with black-skin being
    Fire emeralds in our eyes
      we dance.

   Dawns crawl into long torn moans
    Chilly red-eyed searching howls
    following a path of scattered coals, ash-gray and dead
     Silent huddled moans alone
     rocking on my pelvic bone
      I mourn.

Tonight—a dance.
   wild campfire glowing *risa*
   gritos through its eyes
     Later—scattered coals,
     bitter cold
       and orphaned stumbles, moaning.
       Joy air rippling through free voices.

       Grimace chants of terror
       bleeding broken tears.

       lágrimas and loneliness
       woven through free song of fire
     neither fine wine nor adobe
           yet both

                'and new music.

Porfiria
1986

Porfiria doesn't exist
but if she did
she'd say "¡Que se *chingue* Reagan!"
　　　　"¡Rómpenles el borlote!"
　　　　y "Tráigame una cerveza, Carlos."

Porfiria liked Carlos—like the way he'd take his
pocket knife out, in front of white liberal gringos
and clean his fingernails with it, tryin' to look mean,
tryin' to look like the image of Mexicans they were trying hard
to unbelieve.
Porfiria'd say, not too committed to any one view,
　　　　"Chale, you're okay."

Porfiria didn't like people who were so committed to the
truth they couldn't see anything else.
But Porfiria wasn't prejudiced—she didn't like
people neither who were scared of coming
down hard and being
violently close-minded—saying, like those
wonderful crazy intellectuals visiting
from Latinoamérica would say,
"¡Está usted loco!
¡Cómo puede creer tal cosa!
¡Está completamente equivocado!
¡Es una tontería increíble!"
　　　　She liked that. Took
guts to say it like that, 'steada conference talk,
a la USA, "The distinguished Dr. Satdunk
certainly has a profound comprehension
of the field, but he seems to be forgetting

one major factor, which *could* disprove
his *entire* . . . pardoning my boldness, but . . ."
Porfiria said that was "Chicken shit! Big Mask
                              to hide Little Heart!"
          or the way she put it
          when she was feelin' good: "Paper Prick
                              to hide Bubblegum Huevos."
Porfiria doesn't really exist
but if she did
she'd be the kind to say *"Ya Basta"*
    put a síg-gar in her mouth,
      like Generala Carmen Robles,
        1915 Special, Field General, Mexico-style
          with her men and women standing by her,
    and say quiet, with the smoke blowin' out slow
      every word heavy and dead-eyed

                    "Ya ha comenza'o
                    la revolución."
          and her dead eyes nail you, dying,
              with that unspoken final curse word
                    meanin' "you."

She'd be the kind to get upset about the uptight, lowdown
two-headed academics—one head playing Brown Beret and
dressing ethnic on the Diez y Seis
                    (Veevah luh Rozz-uh, Man!)
other playing bouncing puppy dog
                    (Yes boss! Yes boss!)
can be bought for less than money—
              title, publication,
              mention in the Central Office Minutes . . .
                "Oh, shit!" she'd say,
                  then turn and put a crazy GI hat
                  on and drink beer to German music all night long.

Porfiria'd go home   tired
Apologize to the cat
for not putting her food out on time
                    Say "Chinga'as d'esas fregaderas.
                        Ni me dejan tiempo de prender la vela."

                    "Y ustedes—¿qué?" responds to puppies
                    scrapping, nicknamed Gringo and Chicano,
                    "A lo menos pueden aprender
                    a no cagar en casa ajena." Strokes their necks and
Turns to light the vela
that spiritwarms the house and catches lightdance off a tear
As "Firia" mends her mother's colcha for her,
                    thinking.

Porfiria sat on a few committees
    was quiet a lot
        occasionally mumbled
            and once in a while let loose an
                        "¿Y qué pendejos porqué no?"
                        or even worse a just plain, "Why?"
Got criticized for "lack of finesse"
and answered, for the soflameros,
                    "I handle too much shit
                    to use a dust rag and
                    furniture polish on it.
                    Shovels work just fine."

Porfiria doesn't exist, in the usual way,
    has no photograph, social security number, or signature.
But Porfiria has just so damn much to say
that she will show up anyway, stubborn bitch,
that we will
every one of us

take a picture
    invent a number
    sign a declaration
                for her
    even if it has to be
    with our very own
                names.

La Malinche
1976

Yo soy la Malinche

My people called me Malintzín Tepenal
The Spaniards called me Doña Marina

I came to be known as Malinche
    and Malinche came to mean traitor.

They called me—*chingada*
                    ¡Chingada!

(Ha—¡Chingada! Screwed!)

Of noble ancestry, for whatever that means, I was sold into slavery
by MY ROYAL FAMILY—so that my brother could get my
                                        inheritance.

. . . And then the omens began—a god, a new civilization,
                        the downfall of our empire.
And *you* came.
My dear Hernán Cortés, to share your "civilization"—
                                to play a god,

. . . and I began to *dream* . . .
        I *saw,*
            and I *acted!*

I saw our world
    And I saw yours
        And I saw—
            another.

217

And *yes*—I helped you—
         (against Emperor Moctezuma Xocoyotzín himself!)

I became Interpreter, Adviser, and lover.
    They could not imagine me dealing on a level with you—
        so they said I was raped, used,
               chingada
                ¡Chingada!
But I saw our world
   and your world
      and another.
No one else could *see!*
     Beyond one world, none existed.
    And you yourself cried the night
    the city burned,
      and burned at your orders.
The most beautiful city on earth
            in flames.
You cried broken tears the night you saw your destruction.
My homeland ached within me
              (but I saw *another!*)

Another world—
   a world yet to be born.
And our child was born . . .
   and I was immortalized *¡Chingada!*

Years later, you took away my child
(my sweet mestizo new world child)
    to raise him in your world.
    You still didn't see
      You *still* didn't see.
And history would call *me*
         chingada.

But Chingada I was not.
   Not tricked, not screwed, not traitor.
For I was not traitor to myself—
      I saw a dream
         and I reached it.
            Another world . . .

                  La raza.

                  Ia raaaaaaaa-zaaaaa . . .

Mujeres del rebozo rojo
1995

Who are we,
las mujeres del rebozo rojo,
who are always
waiting for the light
hungry for the pink drops of morning
on the night's sky
searching for the sparkle of creation, of beginning, of life,
on the dawn's burst
trying so hard
to open our eyes

Who are we,
las mujeres del rebozo rojo
who want to reach and stretch and spread
and grow beyond our limits
yawning, pulling up our heads, pushing out our lungs,
arching out our arms
resting only when in growth, transition, transformation
wanting only to be, and to become . . .

    . . . To unfold our lives as if they were a rebozo
        revealing its inner colors,
            the richness of its texture,
            the strength of its weave,
            the history of its making

        Opening to
            all our fullness
            the blossom set free,

Spreading our wings to the reach of the sky
   and awakening
      to who
         we really
            are.

✖ SHEILA ORTIZ TAYLOR

Marker
1987

They said her ashes
were strewn over the desert
from an airplane at sundown
but I could remember photographs
in my dentist's magazine
of glowering FBI agents
shouldering into black cars
pilots whose rose gardens
had been enriched
by their unprotesting clients

In her only recorded comment
on death
my mother leaned across
the Palm Springs breakfast table
we two shared alone
and said of her dead friend
"They put her out like the trash
not a word in the paper, nothing."
Coffee cup to her lips
she stared out the kitchen window
through bougainvillea and grillwork
to desert sand and mountain beyond

One day she turned to bones
on contour sheets.
I flew all day from Florida

changing planes
in every time zone
my watch winding backward

My sister and I sat in shifts
and dripped water into
her open mouth
through straws
while my father crouched
under his desk
selling life insurance
Relieved at sunset
we walked through orange groves
swam together through the darkening pool
listening to the wind
sawing off the limb of night

Once my mother saw girls in white dresses
dancing on the lawn
Next she saw her mother standing
at the foot of her bed, beckoning

But she clung to her kitchen table
said no to her mother
tuned in to *The Price Is Right*
watched through lids
that kept dropping
like storefront
grills

One day she dropped her remote
turned away from Bob Barker
asked, Is that all there is?
Yes, I lied, holding her, drawing her

toward death
like a midwife
pulling a child
toward the light

For days that passed like years
we dripped morphine into her gaping mouth
and wandered through the failing house
while time pulsed through the clocks
and out her veins

Then one night the burglar stood
just beyond her locks
His razor circled the window once
and glass fell out
He stuffed her jewels into pillowcases
slashed photographs with razors
stole the television
and the light

I held her tight
Go to your mother, I said
You go, she answered
and turned away

Next morning I watched her turn into
a spot on the sheet.
We folded her like a flag
and gave her to the pilot

The Way Back
for Uncle Jim
1988

They stand in this Christmas snapshot
poised like adagio dancers
facing each other
their arms draped around
their matching bones
brother and sister
while behind them
out of focus
the family
spins

Around these two
youngest of thirteen
held now for eternity
in this moment before their
twin feet slide them out
in a celestial tango
a silence gathers

We see their handsome faces
Indian bones in glinting cheeks
their raven hair, gray-streaked
their eyes as deep and dark as wells
holding a history of careless loss
land, lovers, mothers, maps

The way back is a land
more innocent than this
He joined the navy
She married a judge

They both baked bread in institutional ovens
He wrote long letters home
and sent his mother silk pillows
embroidered with military targets

He baked bread while
his eight brothers lost fingers
toes, knees, elbows
He could almost hear the bullets
thud into dough
and the sound made him rise
growing from uniform to uniform
until they had to declare peace

Home again
he folded away his whites
kissed his sisters
and told his brothers
he was going to become
a hairdresser
news that made their wounds ache
more than seemed possible
Finally he followed them to work at Lockheed
learned to drill holes in himself
discovered insomnia
married a beautician named Molly
whose hair he dyed green every Christmas

He loved all holidays
Life needed themes
spelled out in sparkles, sprinkles
cutouts, paste-ups
but most of all
in costume.

Halloweens found brother and sister
on their knees
before bolts of cloth
and wimpling tissue
pins in their mouths
blue chalk on their hands
for years
artists of the self

You can see it here
in this snapshot
white polyester pants belling out

around white cowboy boots
red western shirts
tailored close to the rib
Indian silver at the waist
twins in spirit
if not by birth
holding each other
in a light embrace
their grace
not lost

And yet
the way back is a land
more innocent than this
The time came round
when neighbors
preferring razor blades to invention
would not let their children
trick or treat
where a grown man
put costumes on.

That Christmas night
very late
he backed his throbbing
Continental
into the dark garage
that shut down tight behind him
crawled into the backseat
bearing a bottle of champagne
one glass
a photograph

❧ GINA VALDÉS

Spells
1996

You enchant me with a smile of let me
show you the treasures of Oaxaca.

I follow the humming of your dark skin,
to Santo Domingo where under a flamboyán
we sing tender Isthmus songs that swing us
dizzy like Juchitán hammocks.

                Once again
you glide to my house like a forest cloud
with that broad chest that can hold
mountain air and a heart in blossom,
you touch me with those potter's hands
that for centuries have fondled clay
into song.

I taste you in the heat of mezcal,
in the sweetness of orange slices.

               Yes, I whisper,
I will be pulled by this land of spells
where I dare grasshopper tacos, mezcal cedrón,
sway to "Las Nereidas" played on marimba
under a laurel of India, La Zandunga in Zapotec,
spiral into the humming of Monte Albán,
the chiming of ancient dialects, the shout
of el tamalero on Calle Alcalá, the bells

of Santo Domingo, the fragrance of gardenias
and cocoa beans roasting.

                    I can't forget
a mouth electric as the breeze
from the Papaloapan River,
the flutter of bodies and hearts
opening like pumpkin flower.

The Hands
1986

Depending on the light, of the hairy
sun or of the moon, of the shade, of
a tamarind at noon or a chapel at dusk,
the hands, these hands, my hands, your
hands, will appear cream or cinnamon,
pink, red, black, or yellow—our heritage.

These are hands of congas, of requintos,
güiros, claves, bongós and timbales, of
maracas, charangos, guitarrones and marimbas,
castanets, tambourines and cymbals, tin tin
timbaleo tingo, these hands sing, dance,
clap to the beat of corn rumbeando on its way
to becoming a tortilla, these hands round
albóndigas and dreams, circle waists, sighs
and hips, peel bananas, masks, and mangoes,
add, subtract, multiply on blackboards,
beds and griddles, these hands speak fluent
Spanish, they warm, they reduce fevers,
sometimes they write poetry, sometimes
they recite it, these hands could take
away all pain.

These hands, tied by centuries of rope
to ovens, to tables and to diapers, to
brooms, mops, trays and dusters, to saws
and hammers, to picks, hoes and shovels,
they scrub floors, plates and lies, pick
strawberries, grapes, insults and onions,
plant corn, mint, hope and cilantro,
piece by piece they unearth our history.

These hands, so large, so small, two
hummingbirds, quiet, still, joined.
pierced by a nail of U.S. steel, unbind,
shout, close into a fist of sorrow, of
anger, of impatience, these raised hands
open, demand the same as they produce,
as they are giving, these hands smile
in triumph.

❧ GLORIA VANDO

Los Alamos
1979

Why the name? Not a poplar in sight.
Not a sapling, not a songbird.
Not a soul.
In the circular distance
Las Truchas, implacable peaks (second
highest in New Mexico),
secure the sky to the land,
the pueblo bearing their name,
reclining in the hollow of one slope—
waiting, watchful
of the encroaching barrenness below.

Crosses carved from the raw earth
lase lurid warnings across our path,
reminding us, yes, *this is the place*.

We drive past an old adobe hut.
The face of Christ,
painted in a blaze of reds and black
across its whole facade,
looks back at us in pain and disbelief.

> *Los Alamos, Los Alamos,*
> *sacred, secret origin of death—*
> *the name explodes within my head,*
> *dustblood settles on my eyelids, my tongue.*

We slow down, as though searching for something,
something to still the shame.
A sign of hope, of purpose.
Of forgiveness.

Silence. A dry silence. A dusty silence.

And in the shadow of the trading post,
half hidden from the brutal sky,
sullen youngsters damn us with their eyes.

They do not wave as we drive by.

In the Crevices of Night
1981

There's a man in my dream
a man with a hatchet
ransacking my bureau
hacking at the doll asleep
in the bottom drawer.

A bloodless ritual.

He calls himself a surgeon, says
he's up on the latest laser beam
techniques. I know better.
I know the jig's up.
Youth is waning and the end
is closing in on the beginning—
a telescopic fantasy focused
on dismembered limbs, a glass eye
rolling across the parquet floor,
tiny fingernails scattered
in my underwear scratching
at the obscenity of early death.
But not a drop of blood. Not a cry.

I turn from the dream
and pressing my body to yours
reach for you
across the thin ice of night.

Cante Jondo
1989

Segovia says Lorca was killed
by a jealous lover, but I know
that isn't so, I know he was seized
from midnight reverie, pried screaming
from the poem in his head, the lover
beside him pleading with Franco's men
before the butt end of a German carbine
careened him into a wordless sleep
taking him worlds away from Lorca
Guernica and the caves of Andalucía
from the fifth column, the Falange, death
far, far from death, deep into a dream
sweetened by seas, seeping slowly
into Moroccan fields where boys
culipandeando ignite the light-eyed
lust of tourists who come down
to excavate their scraggy yield
Arabs preferring the ripe, moist meat
of melons and Lorca's lover lying
in that crazy hard-on dream, oblivious
of what was going on, unconscious
of his own demise with the poet gone
who would immortalize his soul and
the barrel of a rifle prodding Lorca's
chest like the insistent finger of Uncle
Sam, hard up against his anus, prying
open his mouth *muévelo, maricón* and
Lorca's face green as the craters
of his vellum moon, his body twisted,
a hibiscus against the dawn, stumbles
ahhh! as they jab him on, blindfold

filth across his eyes, *those eyes*, bind
laces from his shoes into his wrists so
when he staggers to the wall his shoes
drag through the gravel, unraveling
the earth's tears, the earth's dark song

drrrggge drrrgge dirige
Domine Deus meus in conspectu tuo . . .

Lorca, my poet, shot down in prayer
while his lover unaware sleeps and dreams
of almond eyes and bougainvillea.
Homosexuals die violent deaths, Segovia
says, playing a Bach fugue on his guitar.

Promesas

1981

To El Santuario de Chimayó,
as to the Ganges, they flock—
the needy, curious, doubting, and devout,
looking for a spiritual handout
from this "most holy national shrine"
(so named under the provisions, mind you,
of the Historic Sites Act of 1935).
They come "to witness, to commemorate
the history of the United States."
United States?—this here's MEXICO, hombre.

And I, the tourist, come too;
to pay homage, to honor—what?
A lost heritage? A dying legacy?
These strangers who speak my tongue
are not *my* people? I'm from Borinquen—
that tiny island drowning in a sea of Coca-Cola.
These people have their *patria*.

An old woman *jesusiando* follows
my pilgrimage into the dank, dark belly
of the sanctuary, her face parched
like the land she is condemned to till,
her fingers flitting from relic
to relic—touching, stroking,
needing to lay hands on her history, to feel
the pulse of her ancestral heart.
The walls are taut with hope and trust;
trinkets everywhere—charms, lockets,
wedding rings with tiny messages of love,
service medals, bracelets, dog tags—all

fabricating a haunting collage of life, death.
Of endurance. Ah yes, endurance.

A cabinet displays photographs of loved ones
with names like the five sons in that old song:
Pedro, Pablo, Chucho, Jacinto, y José; and
letters signed *tu hijo, tu hijita,*
tu marido que te quiere siempre.
Siempre—what a warped and wicked word!
In the center of the room
plastic icons adorned with rosary beads
remind me of deer heads
during the Zuni Shalako—
      turquoise and silver squash blossoms
      wrapped around their slender necks
      to ward off the evil eye of winter—
and in the corners, totemic,
canes and crutches and discarded casts.

And, finally, *promesas*. Tacked to the walls.
Handwritten promises to God:

    This cross is a symbol in thanking you
    for the safe return of my son Juan
    from combat duty in Vietnam.
    I made a promise to walk 150 miles
    from Grants, New Mexico, to Chimayó.

But what if Juan had not come back—what then?
Would his father have dissolved the covenant,
his rage propelling him to curse his God?
Or would he have submitted—
walking farther, seeking deliverance?
It's what my grandfather would have done.

I remember now, I am six, sickly.
My grandfather on his knees beside my bed.
I remember the promised curls
cascading down his chest
and over his vest like a tabard. Once
in a dream, I felt them soft against my cheek
and woke up weeping.

"Kitsch!" quips a man behind me.

The light outside is blinding.

❧ Enedina Cásarez Vásquez

Bad Hair
1992, 1996

I used to sit between *Abuelita*'s legs
On hot summer days
And shed a tear for every yank she gave my hair.
A las niñas siempre se les hacen trenzas,
Así apretaditas
Para que no parezcan pajuelas greñudas
She would say in a raspy old voice
As she wove my hair into long braids
As tight and painful
As the sins I used to confess
At the church of the Apostles Peter and Paul.
And I
Swore that when I grew up
I would cut off all my hair
And suffer no more.
And
When *Apá*
In a drunken stupor
Would take off his black leather belt
To punish me for any offense,
Like
The time I broke a dozen eggs
Or
When I threw up the hamburger I was eating
During one of his fights with *Amá*
Or
Just because he was drunk,

Those times
He would make me stand in the doorway of the
    kitchen
And ask me to walk across the room
While he whipped his belt across my thighs.
It would hurt for a while

Then
I would go into the bathroom
And cut my hair.

Like
During my *mea culpa* days
Growing up Catholic
Thinking that nuns were perfect
And bald.
I wanted to be perfect
And if that meant being bald,
I took pride in cutting my hair
Shorter than my brother's.
Until one day,
As I listened to Sister Cabrini
Tell me that good Catholics
Knew all of the correct answers
In the Baltimore Catechism Manual
And I noticed a strand of hair
Pop out of her starched white veil
Wet with sweat
And how it just hung over her brow
I knew then that some things were not right.
I went home,
I cut my hair.

In college,
During one of those heated war protests

Or
When the students were killed in Mexico City's riots
And *Apá* said they got what they deserved,
Or
When Kennedy was assassinated
On the Thursday I started my period
And I hated all the blood,
Went into my room,
I cut my hair.

And when I wanted to ring the bell
During Sunday Mass
Just like Tony could do,
Dressed in his red altar boy outfit
That I thought would look better on me
And I was told girls were not allowed to ring the
    bells
Or help with communion
Or go near the altar,
I cut my hair.
My braids were pinching my temples,
Giving me headaches.
I wanted to help Father Fitzgerald
Give out the body of Christ
Or hold the Baby Jesus for all to kiss.
I wasn't allowed
Because I was a girl,
Less worthy,
And I believed it.
It has taken a lifetime
To learn I don't have to cut my hair,
That no one will braid my hair again,
That no one will hit me again
And

That if I can't be part of something one hundred
     percent,
I will take my leave because it is not for me.

I will never cut or braid my hair again
I will let it blow in the wind
Color it any color I want
Let it flow down my back
Pin it up to one side
And flaunt it
Because it is mine and I have no bad hair days.

🐘 EVANGELINA VIGIL-PIÑON

apprenticeship
1978

I hunt for things
that will color my life
with brilliant memories
because I do believe
lo que nos dice
la mano del escritor:
that life is remembering

when I join my grandmother
for a tasa de café
and I listen to the stories
de su antepasado
her words paint masterpieces
and these I hang
in the galleries of my mind:

I want to be an artist like her.

corazón en la palma
1996

is it the same muse
whose song
stirred mine—

life was young
even as leaves swirled
I, dizzy
time turning golden

is it the same song
just sung a different way
the melody without its words
how far, far in time
its sadness reaches

bien me dijo mi abuela
nunca sabe uno
lo que viene atrás de los años

lo hondo
1978

entre más nos acercamos
más distante te me haces
guess that's what happens
when two people discover
each other's depths

y hijo,
no sé cuál es más peligroso:
lo hondo
o la corriente

the hands of time
1996

I took the hands of time
held their coolness to my face
squeezed them lightly
turned them both palms up
traveled the lines with my touch
read the mystery
aloud
to remember it
and to fight fear—

s t a r t l e d
I pressed the hands to my chest
swallowing silence
in a gasp

crimson the color
1995

crimson is the color
of a dream:

beam from fierce ball of fire
pierces the frigid darkness of the universe

tender is the touch of a child

pierce through your thoughts
mind streams in explosive directions

conceive in black ink
what you've made of your life
day in and day out
who will, if you won't
tell of the secrets
buried so deeply?

crimson is the color of a dream
peer through the window
ivory roses in full bloom in the backyard
the shocking orange-reds of granada blossoms
the fragile fragrance of nostalgia
dreams and dreams away:

a gold bracelet from a sweetheart
the words inscribed
amorcito consentido

distant planets with no names
    flicker and blink red and blue
in deep vast space

crimson is the color of a dream
delicate the fragrance
fine the bracelet of white gold
soft the touch
rapturous the kiss
distant the dreams

◄ ALMA LUZ VILLANUEVA

Even the Eagles Must Gather
1992

I lay with an acupuncture needle
at the top of my head
and the Berlin Wall goes down—

I lay with an acupuncture needle
in my left hand pulse
and Prague is free—

I lay with an acupuncture needle
in my right hand pulse
and Mandela walks into sunlight—

I lay with an acupuncture needle
in my left foot pulse
and Russia yearns for commercialism—

I lay with an acupuncture needle
in my right foot pulse
and Chile leans toward democracy—

I send my best energy through my body
in spite of the usual human obstacles—
my spirit is too pure for me, as my body
struggles toward its light-streaked path—

but then, my spirit is all I truly trust
and so I entice it back, I say, "Fill me

up with your pure potential—freedom before
death is what I want, the circle—"

It's afternoon, after a storm, wind
that clears dead branches from trees—
the sun sets—the world seeks its freedom
in its own slow way—we kill the enemy,

make love to the enemy, again and again—
it's the way of transcendence. I look out
the window and despise the cars, the circling
traffic and realize, peace in my body;

Even the eagles must gather (to love
the spirit is to love the body—to love
the earth is to love the world—to love
the enemy is to love the self).

Delicious Death

To my son, Marc Jason
1988

Memory: You were fifteen in the mountains,
your friends were going hunting,
you wanted to go.

Cold, autumn day-sky of steel
and rifles, the shades of bullets. We
fought. I didn't want to let you go.

And you stood up to me, "My friends are
going, their parents let them hunt, like
am I some kind of wimp or what, Mom . . ."

We walked into Thrifty's to buy the bullets,
you would use one of their rifles—I imagined
you being shot or shooting another eager boy/man

"What you kill you eat, do you understand?"
I stared each word into your eyes. As you
walked away, I said to the Spirits, "Guard

this human who goes
in search of
lives."

🐚 🐚 🐚

You brought home four small quail.
I took them, saying, "Dinner." I stuffed
them with rice, apples, baked them in garlic,

onions, wine. "Tonight, Mom?" "Yes, tonight."
I plucked the softest tail feathers and as you
showered, I placed them in your pillowcase:

"May the hunter and
the prey be
one.

May the hunter truly
be a human
being.

May the hunter eat
and be eaten in
time.

May the boy always
be alive in the
man."

🐦 🐦 🐦

We ate, mostly, in silence—
I felt you thinking, I just
killed this, what I'm chewing . . .

On the highest peaks the first
powder shines like the moon—
winter comes so quickly.

On your face soft blond hair (yes, this
son is a gringo) shines like manhood—
childhood leaves so quickly.

The wonder of the hunt is on my tongue,
I taste it—wild, tangy, reluctant—
this flesh feeds me well.

I light the candles and thank the quail
in a clear voice—I thank them for their
small bodies, their immense, winged souls.

"God, Mom, you're making me feel like a
killer." "Well, you are and so am I."
Swallowing, swallowing this delicious death.

Warrior in the Sand
1990

I want to be a black belt in
Kung Fu at fifty—

I want to fall in love at fifty,
sixty, seventy, eighty—

I want to wear my bikini (or be
naked) until I die—

I want to dance and sweat at
my pre-death party,

and get drunk on champagne
with my exuberant guests—

and when I've achieved transformation,
I want no crying.

I want laughter. I want someone
to recite my poetry in a loud,
clear voice. I want babies and
children to be in the room, and

I want the poems to mean nothing
to them. I want to peek through
their eyes once before my long,
dangerous journey home. Home

to the spiral that burns with
its terrible, pulsing love.

And let the children laugh with
that recognition before they forget.

It's so easy to forget—
making love, cooking food,
finding shelter, giving birth,
fighting pain, seeking joy.

Will my own children be there—
grandparents by that time—
will I look through my
great-great-grandchildren's

eyes—who knows. I've
insisted they take their freedom
so that I may have mine. Freedom
demands nothing, and love

gives everything. I have
wandered between these
extremes—mountain to ocean,
silence to shout, poet to

woman, counting the stones,
the shells, the feathers in
my pockets, fingering my solitude
as a child runs ahead, singing.

At the edge of the tide, in the
twilight, is a human figure
with arms and legs, a body, a
head, with no particular gender—

a woman/man. Spirals edge its
body, and a spiral is drawn down
the center, where the throat, heart,
lungs, and genitals should be.

Feathers grow from its head.
I laugh with recognition and,
kneeling, plant mine. I place
a perfect, white shell in its

dream-eye. Now I see I was
saving everything for the warrior
in the sand, who will be washed
away by morning.

✍ BERNICE ZAMORA

Contraries
1995

The fury of violins
in the background
do injustice to
the rhythms of
my people's gritos.
Strings burst forth
to depict the aristocrat
on his horse speeding
through the white forest,
away from his mistress's house.
He is racing toward the hour
allotted to his wife.

Voices of my people cry from ravines,
"¡Do not beat the horse, señor!"

Glint
1995

I must write him a letter before he dies.
I would rather send lilies to the only man
who loved this stranger unto herself.
But he prefers songs, or letters.

I know nothing of music.
I failed to listen when he tried to quill notes
we heard together from our separate cells.
Music was no comfort then

and now only as it is embraced by him.

He can't hear well—the toll of beatings,
the desire to age quickly,
the mournful revelation
that he is unloved still.

I must write him a letter before he dies,
translate my diary of those imprisoned years,
learn the secret to singing strangely,
singing from the depths of dungeons.

GLOSSARY OF SPANISH TERMS AND PHRASES

INTRODUCTION

Page xx: *de su antepasado*—of her ancestral past

🐚 **TERESA PALOMO ACOSTA**

The corn tortilla

Line 18: *masa de harina*—corn dough

Line 26: *un poco de esto, un poquito de aquello*—a little of this, a little bit of that

Line 31: *recetas*—recipes

Line 54: *trapito*—cloth

Line 60: *cocinando*—cooking

Line 65: *mija*—my daughter

Line 67: *las mujeres*—the women

In the season of change

Line 8: *bisabuelas*—great-grandmothers

Line 25: *cafecito*—little cup of coffee

Line 26: *chismeando*—gossiping, chewing the rag

Today the pomegranate tree was in bloom

Line 25: *el tío's*—my uncle's

Line 25: *raspas*—shaved-ice cones

It is an exquisite fading away, I think

Line 32: *tejas/aztlán*—Texas/Aztlán, legendary homeland of the Aztecs

261

Line 44:	Y en algunas otras de mis tierras—And in some of my other territories
Line 47:	retratos—paintings
Line 47:	jefes—masters
Line 56:	cuentos—histories
Line 63:	jefe/sujeto/servidor—master/subject/servant

🐚 JULIA ALVAREZ

Homecoming
| Line 2: | finca—country house |

The Dashboard Virgencita
| Title: | Virgencita—Virgin Mary (the suffix cita denotes endearment) |

Audition
Line 26:	novio—boyfriend
Line 29:	guineos—bananas
Line 48:	allamandas—tropical flowers

🐚 GLORIA ANZALDÚA

Cihuatlyotl, Woman Alone
Title:	Cihuatlyotl—woman alone
Line 1:	Raza—My people (mixed blood, Indo-European)
Line 12:	nopalitos—edible tender prickly pear
Line 21:	vecindad familia—neighborhood family

The Cannibal's Canción
| Title: | Canción—song |

La curandera
Title:	La curandera—The woman healer
Line 22:	el sobrino—my nephew
Line 68:	la virgin santísima—the Most Holy Virgin
Line 75:	jacal—hut
Line 98:	yerbitas—herbs
Line 102:	romero—rosemary

Line 114:   *pendejos*—fools
Line 114:   *quelite*—edible weed

🐌 Miriam Bornstein

Una pequeña contribución

Title: *una pequeña contribución*—a small contribution
Line 3:   *rajita de chile jalapeño*—a tiny slice of jalapeño chile (hot pepper)
Line 11:   *le dió sabor*—gave some flavor
Line 12:   *le dió color*—gave some color
Line 13:   *al*—to

🐌 Norma E. Cantú

Trojan Horse

Epigraph: *Ya llegué de donde andaba*—I've come back from where I've been
Line 8:   *Ya ni sé*—I don't even know
Line 9:   *Solo sé que no soy ni una ni la otra*—I only know that I am neither one nor the other
Line 16:   *ne le hace si sí*—no matter whether it's true
Line 17:   *o si no*—or not

Decolonizing the Mind

Line 30:   *mande*—at your service/I await your command

🐌 Ana Castillo

You Are Real as Earth, y Más

Title: *y más*—and more
Line 1:   *ristra*—a string (of dried chiles, garlic, etc.)
Line 2:   *'manito*—little brother
Line 31:   *Tlaquepaque*—town in Mexico, famed for its blown glass and ceramic ware
Line 35:   *Tonantzín*—(our) mother earth, goddess of fertility
Line 35:   *Guadalupe*—Our Lady of Guadalupe/patron saint of the Americas
Line 40:   *farolitos*—luminaries/small lights

Ixtacihuatl Died in Vain

Title: *Ixtacihuatl*—"The Sleeping Woman," one of twin volca-
              noes in Mexico

Line 39::   *Coatlícue*—in Aztec culture, mother of the gods; goddess
              of life and death

Someone Told Me

Epigraph: *Gracias a la vida que me ha dado tanto*—I thank life for all
              its bounty; *me dió dos luceros que cuando los abro*—it gave
              me two eyes (stars) so that I can discern; *perfecto distinguo,*
              lo negro del blanco—the clear difference between black
              and white

Line 2:   *flor de caña*—Flor de Caña, brand name of Cuban rum
              (literally, the cream of the crop)

Line 3:   *Violeta Parra*—Latin American singer and composer

Line 13:   "*Gracias a la vida*"—"Thanks to Life," title of a song by
              Violeta Parra

🐾 ROSEMARY CATACALOS

A Silk Blouse

Line 41:   *henequén*—hemp

Restoration of the Cathedral, San Antonio, Texas

Line 6:   *por ejemplo*—for example

Line 9:   *quinceañeras*—Hispanic girl's coming-of-age event (at age
              fifteen), equivalent to American debut

🐾 LORNA DEE CERVANTES

Beneath the Shadow of the Freeway

Line 31:   *borrachando*—getting inebriated, out on a binge

Bird Ave

Line 5:   *estrolándonos*—strolling

Line 6:   *marchando*—marching

Line 6:   *con missions*—with missions, with a purpose

Line 51:   *flacafeaface*—skinny, ugly face

Line 60:   *sin* class *ni* pomp—without class or pomp
Line 81:   *ganga de*—a gang of

🐾 SANDRA CISNEROS

You Bring Out the Mexican in Me
Line 15:   *navajas*—knives
Line 19:   *mariachi*—a group of troubadour-musicians who perform at weddings, etc.
Line 22:   *berrinchuda, bien-cabrona*—bad-tempered, obstinate bitch
Line 31:   *Popocatepetl / Ixtacihuatl*—twin volcanoes in Mexico
Line 33:   *Agustín Lara*—Mexican song composer of world renown
Line 34:   *barbacoa taquitos*—barbecue tacos
Line 45:   *Me sacas lo mexicana en mi*—you bring out the Mexican in me
Line 53:   *¡Alarma!*—watch out!
Line 67:   *Piñón*—pine nut
Line 71:   *Quiero ser tuya*—I want to be yours
Line 72:   *Quiero amarte. Atarte. Amarrarte*—I want to love you. Bind you. Tie you

With Lorenzo at the Center of the Universe, el Zócalo, Mexico City
Title: *el Zócalo*—plaza, the public square
Line 3:   *la Calle de la Moneda*—Money street
Line 12:   *querida flecha*—dear arrow
Line 45:   *La Hermosa Hortensia*—The Beautiful Hortense

🐾 SILVIA CURBELO

Balsero Singing
Title: *Balsero*—Cuban boat person

🐾 ANGELA DE HOYOS

La Vie: I Never Said It Was Simple
Line 4:   *sentadita muy atenta*—sitting very attentive
Line 7:   *con mi cuchillito*—with my little knife

Lines 17–18:   *Ni soy curandera, con polvitos y milagros, con monitos de aserrín*—nor am I a healer, with magical hocus-pocus and miracles, with little dolls of sawdust

Line 26:   *Llora que llora*—She weeps and she weeps

Line 27:   *¿Por sus hijos?*—For her children?

Lines 28–29:   *Llora porque nunca tuvo hijos. Pobrecita, es yerma. Qué pena.*—She weeps because she *never* had any children. Poor thing, she is barren. What a pity

Line 30:   *por los callejones*—through the alleys

Line 31:   *de San Cuilmas*—of San Cuilmas (a popular nickname for San Antonio)

Lines 40–41:   *Los muñecos y las monadas*—The male dolls and the cutie pies

Line 42:   *Míos. Re-te-míos. Re-que-te-míos!*—Mine. Very mine. Very much mine!

Line 55:   *Huitzilopochtli*—Aztec god of war

Line 70:   *¿Ya ves?*—You see?

For Marsha

Line 29:   *ésta noche, al llegarme*—this very night, as I felt

Line 30:   *la onda de tu poesía*—the empathy of your poetry

Line 31:   *se abrió mi corazón*—the door of my heart opened

Line 32:   *y te descubrí . . . hermana mía*—and I discovered you . . . my sister

🐌 ALICIA GALVÁN

Penance?

Line 1:   *Sor Juana Inés de la Cruz*—Juana de Asbaje, Sister Juana Inés de la Cruz

🐌 VICTORIA GARCÍA-GALAVIZ

Frida in the Nude

Line 1:   *la pendeja*—the foolish woman

Line 8:   *y pintándose*—and applying makeup to her face

Line 10:   *perdida en el espejo*—glued to (lost in) her mirror

Line 21:   *con sus anillos de plata*—with her silver rings

Line 24:   *corazón*—heart
Line 25:   *orgullo*—pride
Line 26:   *nuestra raza*—our (hybrid) race

Malintzín . . . Marina

Title: *Malintzín . . . Marina*—Mexican Indian woman, mistress
             and adviser to Hernán Cortés
Line 20:   *maguey*—cactus (century plant)

🐚 ALICIA GASPAR DE ALBA

La Frontera

Title: *La Frontera*—The Frontier
Line 9:   *sangre*—blood
Line 10:   *y sueños*—and dreams
Line 14:   *lloronas*—weeping women
Line 19:   *Yo también me he acostado con ella*—I too have lain beside
             her

Domingo Means Scrubbing

Line 2:   *trenzas*—braids
Line 11:   *menudo*—Mexican tripe stew
Line 26:   *pisteando*—drinking alcoholic beverages

🐚 CELESTE GUZMÁN

La tía que nunca come azúcar

Line 14:   *y la alemana*—and the German woman
Line 18:   *tío*—uncle
Line 20:   *nomás*—only (corruption of *nada más*)
Line 20:   *reirse*—laughing, to laugh
Line 26:   *Nopalita*—diminutive of *nopal*, a prickly pear
Line 31:   *Pero nosotras sabemos*—but we know
Line 32:   *pan dulcito*—Mexican sweet bread
Line 39:   *tía, que nunca come azúcar*—aunt who never eats sugar

La cama de esperanza

Title: *La cama de esperanza*—the bed of hope
Line 15:   *bruja's*—witch's
Line 16:   *gitanos*—gypsies

🐚 Sheila Sánchez Hatch

Coatlícue

Title: *Coatlícue*—in Aztec mythology, mother of the Gods, goddess of duality, and of birth and death

The Burning God

Line 1:   *Solamente contigo*—Only with you

Line 3:   *y me siento bien*—and I feel just right

Line 5:   *brazos y brazos para más abrazos*—arms and more arms for more hugs

Lines 7–8:   *como que me estoy muriendo*—as if I am dying

Lines 10–11: *una palabra de tus labios sagrados*—one word from your sacred lips

Line 12:   *como la paloma blanca*—like the white dove

🐚 María Limón

cuando se habla de nombres

Title: *cuando se habla de nombres*—when one speaks of names

Line 14:   *los bultos de sus sueños*—the shadows of their dreams

Line 26:   *albañil*—bricklayer, mason

Line 27:   *enjarrador de mercados y teatros*—one who applies (wall) stucco to stores and theaters

Line 50:   *por vida*—for life

🐚 Demetria Martínez

Nativity: For Two Salvadoran Women, 1986–1987

Line 32:   *¿Por qué están aquí?*—Why are you here?

🐚 Pat Mora

La Buena Pastora: The Good Shepherdess

Title: *La Buena Pastora*—The Good Shepherdess

Sonrisas

Title: *Sonrisas*—Smiles

Line 14:   *mucho ruido*—a lot of noise

Curandera

Title:	*Curandera*—Woman Healer
Line 9:	*yerbabuena*—mint

🐌 DEBORAH PARÉDEZ

A Cartography of Passions

Line 12:	*piñones*—pine nuts
Line 18:	*mi cielo mi mar mi luna mi tierra*—my heaven, my sea, my moon, my earth
Line 30:	*la migra*—Immigration Service

Converging Boundary

Line 1:	*Sí, mujeres, sí sabemos*—Yes, ladies, certainly we know
Line 19:	*escritura ellos no pueden decifrar*—literature they cannot decipher

🐌 BEATRIZ RIVERA

Lament of the Terrorist

Line 41:	*Escopeta*—Shotgun

🐌 BEVERLY SÁNCHEZ-PADILLA

Mali

Title:	*Mali*—short version of Malintzín (Doña Marina)
Line 28:	*cacique*—Indian chief
Line 86:	*nomás una de las huercas*—just one of the female brats
Line 87:	*Con ganas*—with spunk
Line 89:	*Una de las cucarachas*—one of the female cockroaches
Line 90:	*Que saben*—who knows
Line 107:	*Pués*—Well
Line 109:	*Nomás una sociedad con*—Just a society with
Line 123:	*mujeres*—women, ladies
Line 138:	*Admira tan lucida cabalgada*—(He) admires such a splendid cavalcade
Line 139:	*y espectáculo tal Doña Marina*—and notable indeed is Doña Marina

Line 140: *India noble al caudillo presentada*—here given to the leader, a noble Indian woman

Line 141: *de fortuna y belleza peregrina*—a pilgrim of fortune and beauty

Line 142: *Con despejado espíritu y viveza*—With clear spirit and liveliness

Line 143: *gira la vista en el concurso mudo*—she turns her eyes to look upon the silent contest

Line 144: *rico manto de extrema sutileza*—(her) rich cloak very understated

Line 145: *con chapas de oro autorizarla pudo*—with locks of gold could authenticate her

Line 146: *prendido con bizarra gentileza*—great is his gallantry for he is attracted

Line 147: *sobre los pechos en ayroso nudo*—to her breasts, covered by a charming knot

Line 148: *reyna parece de la Indiana Zona*—queen-like is she, from the Indian Zone

Line 149: *varonil y hermosísima Amazona*—this worthy and most beautiful Amazon

Line 171: *con bastante fe*—with plenty of faith

🐚 Raquel Valle Sentíes

Laredo

Line 1: *¡Te odio! ¡Te amo!*—I hate you! I love you!

Line 2: *odio*—(I) hate

Line 5: *Amo tus*—I love your

Line 13: *con sus*—with its

Line 16: *la cloaca*—the sewer

Line 22: *raíces*—roots

Line 32: *Odio los cadillos*—I hate the prickly burweed

Line 40: *Pero*—But

Line 41: *mi gente*—my people

Line 42: *a pesar de sus defectos*—in spite of their defects

Line 43: *por sus muchas cualidades*—for their many qualities

Line 44: *que te aman y te odian como yo*—who love you and hate you as I do

CARMEN TAFOLLA

New Song
Line 1:   *lágrimas*—tears
Line 23:   *risa*—laughter
Line 24:   *gritos*—shouts

Porfiria
Line 3:   *Que se chingue*—Screw (Reagan)
Line 4:   *Rómpenles el borlote!*—Break up their act!
Line 5:   *Tráigame una cerveza*—Bring me a beer
Line 21:   *¡Está usted loco!*—You are crazy!
Line 22:   *¡Cómo puede creer tal cosa!*—How can you believe that!
Line 23:   *¡Está completamente equivocado!*—You are totally mistaken!
Line 24:   *¡Es una tontería increíble!*—It is an incredible stupidity!
Line 39:   *Ya Basta*—That's enough
Lines 46–47: *Ya ha comenza'o la revolución*—The revolution has begun
Line 53:   *Diez y Seis*—Sixteen(th) of September
Line 66:   *Chinga'as d'esas fregaderas*—Damn it all
Line 67:   *Ni me dejan tiempo de prender la vela*—They don't allow me time to light a candle
Line 68:   *Y ustedes—¿qué?*—And you—what?
Line 70:   *A lo menos pueden aprender*—At least they can learn
Line 71:   *a no cagar en casa ajena*—to not defecate in someone else's home
Line 80:   *Y qué pendejos porqué no*—And what fools, why not?
Line 83:   *soflameros*—bamboozlers, hypocrites

La Malinche
Title: *La Malinche*—Indigenous woman given to Cortés
Line 6:   *¡Chingada!*—the screwed one

Mujeres del rebozo rojo
Title: *Mujeres del rebozo rojo*—Women Who Wear Red Shawls

SHEILA ORTIZ TAYLOR

The Way Back
Line 2:   *adagio*—graceful ballet

∾ Gina Valdés

Spells
Line 4:   *flamboyán*—a red flamboyant flower

The Hands
Line 7:   *requintos*—A small Mexican guitar
Line 8:   *güiros*—percussion instrument made of a dried gourd
Line 8:   *claves*—percussion instrument used in the folkloric music of the Antilles
Line 8:   *bongós*—bongo drums
Line 8:   *timbales*—kettledrums
Line 9:   *charango(s)*—a kind of five-stringed guitar used by Peruvian Indians
Line 11:   *timbaleo tingo*—the sound made by the hand striking the kettledrums
Line 12:   *rumbeando*—to take a direction (rumbo), to go on a spree
Line 14:   *albóndigas*—meat balls, fish balls

∾ Gloria Vando

Cante Jondo
Line 1:   *Segovia*—Andrés Segovia, a Spanish classical guitarist
Line 1:   *Lorca*—Federico García Lorca, a Spanish poet
Line 15:   *culipandeando*—swaying hips (coined by poet Palés Matos)
Line 27:   *muévelo, maricón*—move it, you homosexual
Line 38:   *Domine Deus meus in conspectu tuo . . ."*—Direct, O Lord my God, my way in thy sight

Promesas
Line 17:   *patria*—motherland
Line 18:   *jesusiando*—praying and crossing oneself (as in Christian faith)
Line 35:   *tu hijo, tu hijita*—your son, your dear little daughter
Line 36:   *tu marido que te quiere siempre*—your husband who loves you always
Line 37:   *Siempre*—Always

🐌 Enedina Cásarez Vásquez

Bad Hair

Line 4:   *A las niñas siempre se les hacen trenzas*—Young girls' hair should always be braided

Line 5:   *Así apretaditas*—Tightly, like this

Line 6:   *Para que no parezcan pajuelas greñudas*—So that they won't look like disheveled delinquent girls of the street

🐌 Evangelina Vigil-Piñon

apprenticeship

Lines 5–6:   *lo que nos dice la mano del escritor*—what (we) are told by the hand of the writer

Line 11:   *de su antepasado*—of her ancestral past

corazón en la palma

Title: *corazón en la palma*—heart in my hand

Line 13:   *bien me dijo mi abuela*—such simple truth my grandmother spoke

Line 14:   *nunca sabe uno*—one never knows

Line 15:   *lo que viene atrás de los años*—the present is blind to our past

lo hondo

Title: *lo hondo*—the depths

Lines 1–2:   *entre más nos acercamos, más distante te me haces*—the closer we get, the more distance there is between us

Lines 6–9:   *y hijo, no sé cuál es más peligroso: lo hondo o la corriente*—and man, I don't know which is worse—the depths or the current

crimson the color

Line 22:   *amorcito consentido*—my favorite / dear little love of mine

NOTES ON HISTORICAL AND MYTHOLOGICAL CHARACTERS

🐾 AZTLÁN

Aztlán is the legendary homeland of the Aztecs. According to their chronicles, they began migrating in A.D. 1168 from a place in the north (somewhere in the southwestern U.S.), and in 1325 they founded their capital, Tenochtitlán. Inasmuch as the indigenous Cochise culture of southern Arizona was the parent culture of the Ute of Colorado, the Pima of Arizona, the Comanche of Texas, the Pueblo of New Mexico, and of many other southwestern tribes who all spoke Uto-Aztecan languages, this and other cultural evidence indicates that the Aztecs as well are direct descendants of the Cochise people.

🐾 COATLÍCUE

Coatlícue, whose name means "the lady of the skirt of serpents," is a very important goddess in the Aztec pantheon. The goddess of earth and fertility, she is the mother of the gods—the sun, the moon, and the stars. She has nursed not only the gods but mankind as well. Thus she is also known as Tonantzín, which means "nuestra madre" (our mother); Teteoinán, "the mother of the gods"; and Toci, "our grand-mother."

🐾 HUITZILOPOCHTLI

In Aztec culture, Huitzilopochtli was the god of war, principal deity of the Mexicans. He represented the rising sun, and his followers, the Aztecs, considered themselves people of the sun, responsible for keeping him alive. They believed that war was a necessary activity, not for conquest but rather to take prisoners, who were used to fulfill the sacred ritual of human sacrifice to the sun.

🐾 FRIDA KAHLO
The wife of famed Mexican muralist Diego Rivera, Frida Kahlo (1907–1954) was an important painter in her own right. Seriously injured in a bus collision, she sublimated her lifelong physical suffering through artistic expression. Her surrealistic paintings, which reveal a highly creative and forceful personality, translate vital episodes of her daily life and also incorporate motifs from the Aztec culture. She is much revered by all Latinos and serves as an important role model for young Chicanas.

🐾 LA LLORONA
The legend of La Llorona is pre-Hispanic in origin. According to Aztec mythology, the goddess Cihuacóatl was the patron of women who had died in childbirth. When they descended to earth at night, weeping and wailing, their fearful ghosts brought bad luck, especially for women and children. The popular Mexican folk tale of La Llorona, "the weeping woman," is actually Cihuacóatl transformed. It is said she carries a cradle or the body of a dead child in her arms. Her ghost usually appears at crossroads, or on a riverbank, moaning and weeping for the loss of her child. In some versions of the story, she drowned her children to keep them from starving to death.

🐾 MALINTZÍN
Malintzín (Doña Marina) was a Mexican woman, a highly intelligent and gifted linguist (fluent in Aztec, Maya, and Spanish), who helped Cortés considerably, especially during his first encounter with Moctezuma. She was the daughter of a coastal noble, and her stepmother sold her into slavery to the Maya, who in turn presented her to Cortés. She became his interpreter, adviser, and mistress. Today in Mexico the name Malinche is a symbol of disloyalty. The term signifies "traitor." See the Introduction for more information on this controversial character.

NOTES ON CONTRIBUTORS

🐇 TERESA PALOMO ACOSTA

A 1993 recipient of the Voertman's Poetry Award from the editors of *New Texas*, Acosta was born and raised in Central Texas. She holds a M.S. in journalism from Columbia University, but has concentrated on Latina studies. She is a lecturer for the Center for Mexican American Studies at the University of Texas at Austin, and was a research associate for the Texas State Historical Association's *New Handbook of Texas*, where she played a significant role in rectifying that important publication's longstanding ethnic oversights.

Acosta's poetry has appeared in *Festival de flor y canto: An Anthology of Chicano Literature*, *In Other Words: Literature by Latinas of the United States*, and *New Texas: An Anthology of Texas Writing*, as well as several journals and literature textbooks.

🐇 MARJORIE AGOSÍN

Born in Bethesda, Maryland, Marjorie Agosín was raised in Chile, the adopted homeland of her Russian and Viennese Jewish great-grandparents and grandparents. The family fled Chile during the madness that pervaded the country just prior to the assassination of President Allende, thereby escaping the ensuing military oppression. Agosín studied in the United States, eventually earning her Ph.D. from Indiana University. A dedicated human rights activist, Agosín has received the Jeannette Rankin Award in Human Rights, the Good Neighbor Award from the Conference of Christians and Jews, and numerous literary and scholarly awards. All of her works reflect her concern for the abuse of human rights throughout Latin America.

Agosín's poetry includes *Conchalí* (1981), *Brujas y algo más/Witches and Other Things* (1984), *Women of Smoke* (1988), *Zones of Pain* (1988), *Hogueras/Bonfires* (1990), *Sargasso* (1993), and most recently, *Toward the Splendid City* (1994). In the latest work, Agosín expands her concerns to a global scale, focusing on several war-ravaged cities around the world and the suffering endured in each. But at the heart of human suffering, Agosín succeeds in finding something indeed splendid—the human heart.

Agosín's collection of prose poems, *Circles of Madness: Mothers of the Plaza de Mayo* (1992), was illustrated with photographs of the mothers of the desaparecidos and other grim scenes from Argentina.

La Felicidad, first published in Santiago, is Agosín's first story collection to be published in English. Translated by Elizabeth Horan, *Happiness* (1994) could easily qualify as magical realism, but Agosín's work goes beyond that shopworn term. As Elena Poniatowska wrote, "Marjorie Agosín could well be the creator of a new fantastic literature in Latin America." Agosín's *A Cross and a Star: Memoirs of a Jewish Girl in Chile* (University of New Mexico Press, 1995) focuses on the life of her mother in the small town of Osorno, Chile, under a generally unknown Nazi regime.

Agosín's latest work is *Tapestries of Hope, Threads of Love: The Arpillera Movement in Chile, 1974–1994* (University of New Mexico Press, 1996).

Agosín creates this new fantastic literature in Massachusetts, where she has taught in the Spanish Department of Wellesley College for the past seventeen years. She is also on the advisory board of *Ms.* magazine.

🐚 JULIA ALVAREZ

The parents of Julia Alvarez, underground opponents of the dictatorship of General Rafael Leónidas Trujillo, were forced to flee the Dominican Republic after their activities became known to Trujillo's secret police. They arrived in New York with their ten-year-old daughter in August 1960. She taught literature for several years before becoming a professor at Middlebury College in Vermont.

Alvarez published her first collection of poetry, *Homecoming*, in 1984. Her second collection was *The Other Side/El Otro Lado* (Dutton, 1995). The publication of *Homecoming: New and Collected Poems* (Plume, 1996) coincided with the New York Public Library's hundredth anniversary exhibit "The Hand of the Poet: Original Manuscripts by 100 Masters, from John Donne to Julia Alvarez."

Her first novel, *How the García Girls Lost Their Accents* (1991), was received with critical acclaim. Named a Notable Book by both *The New York Times* and the American Library Association, it received the PEN Oakland/Josephine Miles Award. The praise lavished on this novel can be summed up in a comment by the *Los Angeles Times*: "Simply wonderful writing."

Alvarez's second novel, *In the Time of the Butterflies* (1994), describes the murder of three heroic sisters under the Trujillo regime. Writing of this story, Sandra Cisneros praised Alvarez for her courage, saying that "all Latinas are indebted to her for resisting the amnesia that has been our history."

¡Yo! (1997) is Alvarez's third novel.

GLORIA ANZALDÚA

Gloria Anzaldúa's ancestors owned land in South Texas from the early eighteenth century through the early twentieth. By the 1930s, however, racist political and legal maneuvering, combined with the drought of that era, had reduced the family to sharecropping. Anzaldúa was born near the old family lands in Raymondville, Texas. She attended Pan American University in Edinburg, Texas, and received her M.A. from the University of Texas at Austin. She recently received her Ph.D. from the University of California at Santa Cruz, where she has lived for several years.

Perhaps the foremost Latina lesbian writer of the 1980s and '90s, Anzaldúa co-edited with Cherríe Moraga the important anthology *This Bridge Called My Back: Radical Writings by Women of Color* (1981), recipient of the Before Columbus Foundation's American Book

Award. In 1987, Anzaldúa published something of a magnum opus, *Borderlands/La Frontera: The New Mestiza*, an insightful collection of memoir, essay, poetry, and folklore that reflects her lifelong experience of living between cultures. Both *This Bridge Called My Back* and *Borderlands/La Frontera* are core works, essential to understanding the development of Latina feminist literature. Anzaldúa has also edited *Making Face, Making Soul/Haciendo Caras: Creative and Critical Perspectives by Women of Color* (1990) and an issue of *SIGNS: Journal of Women in Culture and Society*, entitled "Theorizing Lesbian Experience" (1993).

Anzaldúa is also the author of two children's books, *Prietita Has a Friend/Prietita tiene un amigo* (1991) and *Prietita Encounters La Llorona* (1995).

⏀ MIRIAM BORNSTEIN

Miriam Bornstein is a poet and critic whose literary/creative voice emerges by preference in Spanish, because she says "not only is the Spanish language my maternal tongue, the one that defines me far better than does the English, it also serves as a strong bond with my culture by way of a feminine perspective—it becomes my ID as I navigate in the Anglo-Saxon Puritan world."

Born in Puebla, Mexico, to a Mexican mother and a Polish father, she has lived in the United States since 1964. After obtaining her Ph.D. from the University of Arizona, she became assistant professor in the Department of Languages and Literatures at the University of Denver, where she presently teaches Chicano and Latin American literature and culture.

She has published two books of poetry, *Bajo Cubierta/Under Cover* (1976, Scorpion Press) and the recent *Donde Empieza la Historia/ Where the Story Begins* (1993, Spanish Press).

Her poetry has been published in literary magazines, such as *Letras Femeninas*, *Revista Chicano-Riqueña* and *Areíto*, and appears in national and international anthologies, including *Latina Creative Literature: An Anthology of Hispanic Women Writers*; *Siete Poetas, Nosotras: Latina Literature Today, Chicano Literature Written in Spanish, La Voz Urgente: Antología de Literatura Chicana en Español, Infinite Divisions:*

An *Anthology of Chicana Literature*, and most recently, *Daughters of the Fifth Sun*.

In the field of literary criticism, Bornstein's work focuses on literature by Chicanas, particularly that of Chicana poets, the contemporary sociopolitical Latin American poetry, and feminist theory. Her essays have appeared in *Revista Casa de las Américas*, *Cuadernos Americanos*, *La Palabra*, and *The Denver Quarterly*.

🐌 GIANNINA BRASCHI

Born in San Juan, Puerto Rico, Giannina Braschi lived in several European capitals before settling in New York, where she earned her Ph.D. in Hispanic literatures from SUNY in 1980. She has taught at Rutgers University and City University of New York, and in 1997 will be the Distinguished Writer in Residence at Colgate University.

Braschi's books include *Asalto al Tiempo* (Barcelona, 1981), *La Poesía de Becquer* (Mexico City, 1982), *El Imperio de los Sueños* (Barcelona, 1988), and *La Comedia Profana* (Barcelona, 1988). Her collected works, translated into English by Tess O'Dwyer, were published as *Empire of Dreams* (Yale University Press, 1994). Her work regularly appears in anthologies of Latin American writing as well as in such standards as the new *Contemporary American Poetry*.

Urbane, sophisticated, and witty, Braschi's work "challenges the borders of genre and language by cross-dressing poetry as theater, story, commercial, tabloid, confession, musical and manifesto."

🐌 NORMA E. CANTÚ

Norma Cantú is a native of *la frontera*, born in Nuevo Laredo, Tamaulipas, a fact that colors all her writing and is the inspiration for much of her research. Cantú is a leading scholar in Chicana literature as well as in folklore and cultural studies. She recently returned to her position as professor of English at Texas A&M International University in Laredo, Texas, after serving as senior arts specialist at the National Endowment for the Arts in Washington, D.C.

Twice a Fulbright research fellow, she recently received a Rockefeller research fellowship, administered through the Guadalupe Cultural Arts Center's Gateways Program, for which Cantú is conducting an ethnographic study of *la quinceañera* as it is practiced in South Texas and northern Mexico.

Cantú was on the editorial team that produced *Chicana Voices: Intersections of Race, Class, and Gender* (Center for Mexican American Studies, 1986), an important work in Chicana studies. She is the 1996 Premio Aztlán recipient for her *Canícula: Snapshots of a Girlhood en la Frontera* (University of New Mexico Press, 1995). Cantú calls *Canícula* a "creative autobioethnography" that chronicles her growing up in los dos Laredos. Her latest book, *Soldiers of the Cross: Los Matachines de la Santa Cruz*, was published by Texas A&M University Press in 1997.

🐾 ANA CASTILLO

Novelist, poet, editor, translator, and coiner of the term *xicanisma*, Ana Castillo is the author of four collections of poetry: *Otro Canto* (1977), *The Invitation* (1979), *Women Are Not Roses* (1984) and *My Father Was a Toltec* (1988, rev. ed. 1995).

Castillo's first novel, *The Mixquiahuala Letters* (1986), received an American Book Award from the Before Columbus Foundation and was selected by the National Endowment for the Arts for presentation at book fairs in Frankfurt and Buenos Aires. *Sapogonia* (1988) was a sprawling political novel that showed Castillo's tremendous scope of interest. But it was *So Far from God* (1993) that brought Castillo a national reputation and critical acclaim. Her latest work is a collection of short stories entitled *Loverboys* (1996).

Castillo is also author of a collection of essays, *Massacre of the Dreamers: Essays on Xicanisma* (1994), and editor of a collection of stories, poems, and essays about Our Lady of Guadalupe, *La Diosa de las Américas/Goddess of the Americas* (1996).

Clarissa Pinkola Estés, author of *Women Who Run With the Wolves*, has written that Castillo "is immensely insightful in every sense of the word. Her work, anything and everything written by her . . . must be read if one is to gain understanding of the vast landscape of soul and life lived with vitality."

A native of Chicago, Castillo has lived, studied, and taught all over the United States and Europe. She has received a National Endowment for the Arts fellowship and was recently recognized for "outstanding contributions to the arts" by the National Association of Chicano Studies.

🐌 ROSEMARY CATACALOS

Born in San Antonio, Texas, Rosemary Catacalos brings to her poetry elements of both her Mexican and Greek ancestry to create an entrancing and often mythic fusion. The title of her first book, *As Long As It Takes* (1984), a fine letterpress chapbook, says a lot about her approach to writing, which is characterized by lengthy gestation periods and extreme attention to craft. Her second book, *Again for the First Time* (1985), received the Texas Institute of Letters Poetry Prize.

Catacalos has received five Pushcart Prize nominations and a special mention in Pushcart Prize IX. She was awarded a 1985 Dobie Paisano Fellowship by the University of Texas at Austin and the Texas Institute of Letters, and was a Stegner Creative Writing Fellow in Poetry at Stanford University, 1989–1991, where she received the Patricia Smith Poetry Prize. She also received a National Endowment for the Arts fellowship in poetry. One of Catacalos's poems was selected by Adrienne Rich for inclusion in *Best American Poetry 1996*.

A former newspaper reporter and columnist, Catacalos devoted herself to various poets-in-school projects for over a decade. From 1986 to 1989, she was the literature program director for the Guadalupe Cultural Arts Center, where she developed the San Antonio Inter-American Bookfair into the major literary event in the Southwest.

Catacalos has served extensively on grant review and policy development panels for the National Endowment for the Arts, several state commissions on the arts, and other organizations, including the Council of Literary Magazines and Presses and the Lila Wallace–Reader's Digest Fund. From 1991 to 1996, Catacalos was executive director of the Poetry Center and American Poetry Archives at San Francisco State University. She currently holds a two-year appointment as an affiliated scholar of the Stanford Institute for Research on Women and Gender.

🐚 LORNA DEE CERVANTES

A fifth-generation Californian of Mexican and Native American (Chumasch) heritage, Lorna Dee Cervantes has been a pivotal figure in the Chicano literary movement since the mid-1970s, when she began publishing *Mango*, a literary journal. Her small publishing company, also named Mango, published several important chapbooks, including the first books of Sandra Cisneros, Gary Soto, Luis Omar Salinas, and Alberto Rios. Cervantes is a dynamic poet whose work draws tremendous power from her struggles in the literary and political trenches. Her power is channeled by a keen intellect and careful craft, which allows her to explore the boundaries between language and experience. Cervantes's first book, *Emplumada* (University of Pittsburgh, 1981), was praised as "a seamless collection of poems that move back and forth between the gulf of desire and possibility." Her second collection, *From the Cables of Genocide: Poems on Love and Hunger* (Arte Público, 1991), was awarded the Patterson Poetry Prize and the poetry prize of the Institute of Latin American Writers. She holds an A.B.D. in the history of consciousness. After completing a year-long visiting scholar fellowship at the University of Houston, she has recently returned to the University of Colorado in Boulder, where she teaches creative writing. Cervantes is a founding co-editor of *Red Dirt*, a literary magazine. She has received two National Endowment for the Arts poetry fellowships.

🐚 LISA CHÁVEZ

Chicana/Native American/Norwegian poet Lisa D. Chávez was born in Los Angeles but raised in Fairbanks, Alaska. She is currently finishing her Ph.D. in American literature at the University of Rochester. A veteran of the Peace Corps, Chávez has taught in Japan, Poland, and at several U.S. universities. Chávez's poetry has appeared in numerous literary magazines, including *Calyx, Sing Heavenly Muse!*, and *Tsunami*. A collection of her poems, *Destruction Bay*, is forthcoming (1998) from West End Press.

Much of Chávez's work is cast as dramatic monologues, which explore women's lives in harsh and dramatic landscapes.

🐌 SANDRA CISNEROS

A truly international figure, Sandra Cisneros is the leading U.S. Latina writer in the world in terms of sales, visibility, and critical reception. Born in Chicago, Cisneros received her M.F.A. from the University of Iowa Writers Workshop. She has lived in San Antonio (off and on) since 1984, when she became the director of the literature program for the Guadalupe Cultural Arts Center. In 1985 she co-founded with Bryce Milligan the Annual Texas Small Press Bookfair, the forerunner of the Inter-American Bookfair. Extremely popular as a lecturer and creative writing teacher, Cisneros has been a writer in residence at universities all over the United States.

Cisneros has received two National Endowment for the Arts fellowships, one in fiction and one in poetry, a Dobie-Paisano fellowship, and numerous other honors, including an honorary Doctor of Letters degree from the State University of New York at Purchase and a MacArthur Foundation fellowship.

The author of three collections of poetry and two of short fiction, Cisneros's books have been translated into ten languages. Her poetry is collected in *Bad Boys* (1980), *My Wicked Wicked Ways* (1987, reissued 1992), and *Loose Woman* (1994). At the invitation of poet laureate Gwendolyn Brooks, Cisneros read her poetry at the Library of Congress in 1986; in 1995 she returned at the invitation of poet laureate Rita Dove.

The House on Mango Street, long one of Arte Público's best-selling titles, was republished by Vintage in 1991. A tenth-anniversary edition in hardback and a Spanish edition, translated by Elena Poniatowska, were published in 1994.

Cisneros's *Woman Hollering Creek* (1991) was awarded the PEN Center West Award for fiction, the Quality Paperback Book Club New Voices Award, the Anisfield-Wolf Book Award, and the Lannan Foundation Literary Award, and was selected as a noteworthy book by several major U.S. newspapers.

Cisneros is currently at work on a novel entitled *Caramelo*.

JUDITH ORTIZ COFER

Judith Ortiz Cofer was born in Hormigueros, Puerto Rico, the daughter of a navy man who moved his family back and forth between the island and Paterson, New Jersey. The family moved to Augusta, Georgia, in 1968. Ortiz Cofer attended high school and college in Augusta, then earned her M.A. at Florida Atlantic University. She also did graduate work on scholarship at Oxford University.

Ortiz Cofer began writing poetry after college. After four early chapbooks were published, two full-length collections, *Reaching for the Mainland* and *Terms of Survival*, both came out in 1987. Her poems have been widely anthologized.

Silent Dancing: A Remembrance of a Puerto Rican Childhood (1990) received a PEN American/Albrand special citation and was named a Best Book for the Teen Years by the New York Public Library. The title essay was included in the *1991 Best American Essays* anthology, edited by Joyce Carol Oates. Another essay included in this collection, "More Room," was included in the Pushcart Prize anthology.

Ortiz Cofer's autobiographical novel, *The Line of the Sun* (1990), is based on her family's "gradual immigration" to the United States. *The New York Times Book Review* hailed the author as "a writer of authentic gifts, with a genuine and important story to tell."

The Latin Deli: Prose and Poetry was published in 1993 to critical acclaim and received the Anisfield-Wolf Award. "Nada," from *The Latin Deli*, received an O. Henry Award in 1994. Ortiz Cofer's latest work is *An Island Like You: Stories of the Barrio* (1995).

Currently, Ortiz Cofer is a professor of English and creative writing at the University of Georgia and an associate staff member of the Bread Loaf Writers Conference.

LUCHA CORPI

Lucha Corpi was born in Jáltipan, Veracruz, Mexico, spent her teens in San Luis Potosí, and emigrated to the United States with her husband at the age of nineteen. Very shortly, she was actively involved in the Chicano movement, becoming both vice-chair of the Chicano Studies Executive Committee and coordinator of the Chicano Studies

Library in 1970 at the University of California at Berkeley. She was a founding member of Aztlán Cultural.

Corpi's poetry was first collected in *Fireflight: Three Latin American Poets* (1976). Corpi's translator in that book, Catherine Rodríguez-Nieto, has since worked with the poet to produce two more award-winning collections, *Palabras de mediodía/Noon Words* (1980) and *Variaciones sobre una tempestad/Variations on a Storm* (1990). While Corpi writes her poetry in Spanish, all of her fiction has been written in English. The novels *Delia's Song* (1984) and *Eulogy for a Brown Angel* (1992) are both set in turbulent early days of the movimiento in California. *Eulogy* features one of Latina literature's only detectives, Gloria Damasco, who has reappeared in Corpi's latest novel, *Cactus Blood* (1995).

🔊 SILVIA CURBELO

Born in Matanzas, Cuba, Silvia Curbelo emigrated to the United States at the age of twelve in 1967. She has received poetry fellowships from the National Endowment for the Arts, the Florida Arts Council, the Cintas Foundation, and the Atlantic Center for the Arts. In 1992 she was co-winner of the James Wright Poetry Prize from *Mid-American Review*. She is the author of *The Geography of Leaving* (Silverfish Review Press, 1991) and *The Secret History of Water* (Anhinga Press, 1997). Her work has appeared in magazines such as *American Poetry Review*, *Kenyon Review*, *Prairie Schooner*, and *Indiana Review*, and in several anthologies, including *Currents from the Dancing River* and *Paper Dance: 55 Latino Poets*. Her poem "If You Need a Reason" was awarded the 1996 Jessica Nobel-Maxwell Memorial Poetry Prize from *American Poetry Review*. Curbelo lives in Tampa, Florida, where she works as an editor for *Organica Quarterly*.

🔊 ANGELA DE HOYOS

Angela de Hoyos was born in Coahuila, Mexico, and has lived most of her life in San Antonio, Texas. Extremely affected by the Chicano political movement in the late 1960s and early 1970s, and especially by the plight of Texas farm workers in solidarity with the unionization activities of César Chávez in California, De Hoyos's early poems were very political. In fact, her work is often cited as among the first fruits of the Chicano literary movement. Her books include *Arise Chicano! and Other Poems* (1975), *Chicano Poems: For the Barrio* (1975), *Poems/Poemas* (Buenos Aires, 1975), *Selecciones* (Xalapa, 1976), *Selected Poems/Selecciones* (1977), and *Woman, Woman* (1985). De Hoyos's poems have appeared in hundreds of literary magazines, dating to the very beginnings of the Chicano literary movement in the late 1960s, and in dozens of anthologies, including the *Longman Anthology of World Literature by Women*.

De Hoyos's poetry has been honored with awards in Argentina, India, Italy, Germany, and the United States. Her work has been the subject of well over a hundred reviews in a dozen different countries. In Europe, she is one of the best known of all U.S. Latina writers, where her work has been the subject of several Ph.D. dissertations in Germany and Italy. Her work has been translated into fifteen languages. In this country, two book-length studies of her work have been published: *The Multifaceted Poetic World of Angela de Hoyos* (1985) by Marcella Aguilar-Henson and *Angela de Hoyos: A Critical Look* (1979) by Luis Arturo Ramos.

Recent honors include recognition by the National Association of Chicano Studies in 1993 for her contributions to Chicano letters, and a 1996 lifetime achievement award from the Guadalupe Cultural Arts Center.

De Hoyos has been a crucial force in Chicano letters as the publisher/editor of M&A Editions, and of *Huehuetitlan*, a well-regarded if small poetry/Chicano culture journal. She is also a painter and graphic artist.

De Hoyos's most recent work was as a co-editor of *Daughters of the Fifth Sun: A Collection of U.S. Latina Fiction and Poetry* (Putnam/ Riverhead Books, 1995).

❧ ROSARIO FERRÉ

Rosario Ferré was born in Ponce, Puerto Rico. She obtained her Ph.D. from the University of Maryland in Latin American literature, but her literary career began long before in 1970, when she started what would become Puerto Rico's most important literary magazine, *Zona de carga y descarga*. After her first book of short stories, *Papeles de Pandora*, appeared (1976), Ferré became the literary critic for *El Mundo*. She is known as an insightful literary critic and has held visiting professorships at the University of California at Berkeley, Johns Hopkins University, Rutgers University, and elsewhere. Several of Ferré's twenty-plus books have been published in Mexico, including *Sitio a Eros* (1982), a collection of feminist essays, *Fábulas de la garza desangrada* (1984), a collection of poetry, and *Maldito Amor* (1986), a novel, which Ferré translated into English and published in the United States as *Sweet Diamond Dust* (1989). "The Glass Box," included in *Daughters of the Fifth Sun*, is from Ferré's short story collection, *The Youngest Doll* (1991). A novel, *The House on the Lagoon* (1995), was called by Elena Poniatowska "a pivotal work in Latin American literature." *The Washington Post* declared Ferré "one of Latin America's most gifted novelists," comparing her with Gabriel García Márquez and Isabel Allende.

🐚 ALICIA GALVÁN

Poet, artist, and pharmacist Alicia Galván was born in Michigan and raised in San Antonio, Texas. She is a respected west side San Antonio businesswoman and the author of three volumes of poetry, *Parenthesis* (1994), *Enigma* (1995), and *Eclipse* (1995). Galván is a board member of the Women's Caucus for the Arts and is active in numerous other regional arts and literary organizations.

🐚 VICTORIA GARCÍA-GALAVIZ

Victoria García-Galaviz won first place in the regionally televised (PBS) 1995 poetry slam sponsored by the Guadalupe Cultural Arts Center. Also through the Guadalupe, she has studied creative writing in master classes with Pat Mora, Gary Soto, Joy Harjo, and Sandra Cisneros. Her work has appeared in several literary magazines and in *This Promiscuous Light: Young Women Poets of San Antonio* (1996). García-Galaviz was the subject of a feature story on new Latina poets in the *San Antonio Express News*, and has been interviewed on National Public Radio. She is a student at the University of Texas at San Antonio, where she is studying literature and creative writing.

🐚 ALICIA GASPAR DE ALBA

Raised a few miles from the Córdoba Bridge in El Paso, Texas, Alicia Gaspar de Alba began publishing her stories in elementary school. She studied creative writing with James Ragan, Raymond Carver, and Leslie Ullman. She holds a Ph.D. in American studies from the University of New Mexico. She has published poems and stories in magazines such as *Revista Chicano-Riqueña, Imagine: International Chicano Poetry Journal, Common Lives/Lesbian Lives,* and *Puerto del Sol* and in numerous anthologies. Gaspar de Alba was one of three poets included in *Three Times a Woman* (Bilingual Review Press, 1989). She is the author of a collection of short stories, *The Mystery of Survival and Other Stories* (Bilingual, 1993). She currently lives in Claremont, California, where she is working on a novel on Sor Juana Inés de la Cruz. A scholarly work, entitled *Chicano Art Inside/Outside the Master's House,* will be published in 1998 by the University of Texas Press. Gaspar de Alba is a professor of Chicana/Chicano Studies at UCLA.

🐚 CELESTE GUZMÁN

Celeste Guzmán's poetry has appeared in regional literary magazines and in *This Promiscuous Light: Young Women Poets of San Antonio* (1996). She graduated in 1997 with a double major in English and theater from Barnard College in New York, where she studied playwriting with Steve Friedman. She was a Barnard Centennial Scholar and the winner of the 1995 National Hispanic Scholarship. Guzmán's first play, "Burnt Sienna," won the 1996 American College Theater Festival's Ten-Minute Play Award. She currently works as a grants writer for the Guadalupe Cultural Arts Center in San Antonio, Texas.

🐚 SHEILA SÁNCHEZ HATCH

San Antonio poet and short story writer Sheila Sánchez Hatch has published work in several literary magazines and anthologies, including *Linking Roots* (1993), *Mujeres Grandes I* (1993), and *Daughters of the Fifth Sun* (1996). Sánchez Hatch edited a collection of work by North Texas Latinos, *Tierra Norte* (1994). She holds a MFA from Vermont College and has taught English for the Alamo Community College District in San Antonio and creative writing for the Guadalupe Cultural Arts Center. She is currently writer in residence with the San Antonio Independent School District. Hatch's latest work, a collection of fiction and poetry, is *Guadalupe and the Kaleidoscopic Screamer* (Wings Press, 1996).

🐍 MAYA ISLAS

Maya Islas was born in Cabaiguán, Las Villas, Cuba, and she came to the United States in 1965. In 1978 she received her M.S. in general psychology from Montclair State College. She has been a bilingual teacher in the public schools of New York City, writer in residence at the School of Design, Altos de Chavón, Dominican Republic, and a counselor for the Higher Education Opportunity Program at Elizabeth Seton College in New York.

Islas co-founded, along with José Corrales and Mireya Robles, the literary magazine *Palabras y Papel* in 1981. She has published several books of poetry, including *Merla* (1971), *Without a Name* (1974), *Shadows-Paper* (1978), *Hubo la viola* (1979), *Altazora Accompanying Vincent* (1989), and *Blackbird* (Madrid, 1991). She received the Silver Caravelle Award in Poetry (1978), from Barcelona, for the poem "Words of the Dove"; the 1986 Gold Letters Award from the University of Miami for her book *Altazora Accompanying Vincent;* and the 1993 Latino Literature Prize in Poetry for her book *Blackbird.*

🐍 MARÍA LIMÓN

Born and raised in El Paso, Texas, María Limón currently works with the Foundation for a Compassionate Society in Austin, Texas. Her poetry began appearing in regional literary magazines and chapbooks in the mid-1980s. A short story is included in *Entre Guadalupe y Malinche* (1997). She has studied creative writing with Joy Harjo and Sandra Cisneros through the Guadalupe Cultural Arts Center's master classes.

🐍 RITA MAGDALENO

Born in Germany and raised in Phoenix, Arizona, Rita Magdaleno recently returned to the land of her birth to lecture on Chicano literature at the universities of Augsburg and Bamberg. Magdaleno has been awarded fellowships at various writing colonies including Millay and Ucross, and has taught at the University of Maryland, the University of Arizona, and Pima Community College. When not lecturing elsewhere, she lives in Tucson, where she is an artist in the schools and a commissioner on the board of the Arizona Commission on the Arts.

Her poetry and fiction has appeared in numerous literary magazines, and in anthologies such as *New Chicana/Chicano Writing* (1993), *After Aztlán: Latino Poets of the '90s* (1994), *Walking the Twilight: Women Writers of the Southwest* (1994), and in *Neueste Chicano-Lyrik: Recent Chicano Poetry* (1994).

🐎 DEMETRIA MARTÍNEZ

The first and only U.S. journalist to be prosecuted for working with the sanctuary movement during the 1980s, Demetria Martínez is one of the few poets in the United States ever to have one of her own poems produced in evidence against her. That poem, "Nativity: For Two Salvadoran Women," is included in this anthology.

Born in Albuquerque, New Mexico, Martínez is a graduate of Princeton University's Woodrow Wilson School of Public and International Affairs. Martínez has been a reporter, editor, and columnist for the *National Catholic Reporter* since 1985. Currently she lives and works in Tucson, Arizona.

Martínez won first prize for poetry in the fourteenth annual Chicano Literary Contest (University of California, Irvine). A collection of her poems entitled "Turning" was included in the anthology *Three Times a Woman*. Her latest work, a lyrical political novel entitled *Mother Tongue* (Bilingual Press, 1994; Ballantine, 1996), received the Western States Book Award for Fiction. John Nichols called her "one of the best, most poetic, and most passionate writers of her generation."

🐎 BRYCE MILLIGAN

Bryce Milligan is the author of five novels and short story collections for young adults, five produced plays, three volumes of poetry, and over fifteen hundred articles and reviews. Milligan's most recent volume of poetry, *Working the Stone*, was compared by E. A. Mares in *The Texas Observer* to the work of Seamus Heaney and Donald Hall.

Milligan is currently the literature program director of the Guadalupe Cultural Arts Center, one of the largest and oldest Latino arts centers in the country. His association with the center began in 1984 when, as the editor of *Pax: A Journal Through Culture*, he co-founded with Sandra Cisneros the First Annual Texas Small Press Bookfair, now the San Antonio Inter-American Bookfair and Literary Festival. Milligan is the founding director of "Hijas del Quinto Sol: Studies in Latina Identity and Literature," an annual academic conference co-sponsored by the Guadalupe Cultural Arts Center and Saint Mary's University in San Antonio. He is also one of the three editors of *Daughters of the Fifth Sun: A Collection of Latina Fiction and Poetry* (Putnam/Riverhead, 1995). He is the publisher/editor of Wings Press, which publishes a Chicana Chapbook series.

Milligan is one of several editors of a CD-ROM on U.S. Latino history, *American Journeys: The Hispanic Experience* (Primary Source Media, 1995), and the author of the Tejana chapter in *Texas Women Writers* (Texas A&M University Press, 1997).

🐌 MARY GUERRERO MILLIGAN

A native of San Antonio, Mary Guerrero Milligan received her MLS from the University of North Texas. A private school librarian, she regularly presents programs and workshops on multicultural children's literature at conferences around the country and for regional librarians and teachers.

Guerrero Milligan has also been a freelance researcher, indexer, and cataloguer, and has long served as the children's manuscript reader/editor for Corona Publishing Company of San Antonio. She has written reviews for various newspapers, literary magazines, and small journals. She was a regular essayist, translator, and interviewer for the journal *Pax*.

Guerrero Milligan's short stories have appeared in *Blue Mesa Review* and *Huehuetitlan*, *Mujeres Grandes I*, and *Mujeres Grandes II*. Guerrero Milligan is a co-editor of *Daughters of the Fifth Sun: A Collection of Latina Fiction and Poetry* (Putnam/Riverhead, 1995).

Guerrero Milligan has been married to novelist/poet/critic Bryce Milligan for twenty-three years. They live in downtown San Antonio in a hundred-year-old home with their two children, two cats, and 15,000 books.

🐾 PAT MORA

The poet of the great Chihuahuan desert, Pat Mora was born and raised in El Paso, where she lived, taught, and served in various top administrative capacities at the University of Texas at El Paso until moving to Cincinnati, Ohio, in 1989. A Kellogg Leadership Fellowship in 1986 allowed her to study cultural conservation issues nationally and internationally. Called the "most widely anthologized Latina poet in this country," Mora and her work have received numerous awards and honors, including two Southwest Book Awards and a National Endowment for the Arts poetry fellowship. Mora's poetry collections include *Chants* (1984), *Borders* (1986), *Communion* (1991), *Agua Santa/Holy Water* (1995), and *Aunt Carmen's Book of Practical Saints* (1997). She is also the author of two important collections of personal essays, *Nepantla: Essays from the Land in the Middle* (1993) and *House of Houses* (1997). She is rapidly becoming a major children's author, with titles such as *A Birthday Basket for Tía* (1992), *Listen to the Desert: Oye al desierto* (1994), *Pablo's Tree* (1994), *The Desert Is My Mother* (1994), *A Gift of Poinsettias* (1995), and *The Race of Toad and Deer* (1995).

🐾 TESS O'DWYER

Translator Tess O'Dwyer received the Columbia University Translation Center Award for her translation of the collected works of poet Giannina Braschi, entitled *Empire of Dreams* (Yale University Press, 1996). Her translations have appeared in several major magazines and journals. She is currently translating the nineteenth-century novel *Martín Rivas* by Alberto Blest Gana for Oxford University Press. O'Dwyer lives in New York City.

🐾 ELVIA PADILLA

Raised near the Ysleta Pueblo outside of El Paso, Texas, Elvia Padilla is currently pursuing her M.A. in creative writing and Chicano studies at the University of Texas at Austin. She has also studied poetry with Joy Harjo in a Guadalupe Cultural Arts Center master class. Her work has garnered college writing contest awards and appeared in *Interrace Magazine* and others.

🐚 ANABELLA PAIZ

Born in Guatemala City, Guatemala, Anabella Paiz holds both a M.A. and M.F.A. from the University of Miami. She is a translator, poet, and short story writer, and her work has appeared in *Prairie Schooner, Mangrove, Conjunctions*, and other literary magazines.

🐚 DEBORAH PARÉDEZ

Deborah Parédez, a native of San Antonio, has been publishing her poetry in literary magazines, large and small, since the age of fifteen. As a very young writer, she was included several times in the *Young Pegasus* anthology, the oldest student poetry publication in the United States. She attended Trinity University, where she was selected to edit the university literary magazine. During a year's stay in Seattle, she worked as an intern on the *Crab Creek Review* and began independent studies on Latina literature. Her poetry has appeared in *Daughters of the Fifth Sun: A Collection of U.S. Latina Fiction and Poetry* (Putnam, 1995) and in *This Promiscuous Light* (Wings Press, 1996). A gifted actress with a taste for the absurd, Parédez is currently working on her Ph.D. in Latino theater at Northwestern University.

🐚 TERESINKA PEREIRA

Born in Belo Horizonte, Brazil, Teresinka Pereira has lived in the United States since 1960. An international figure, she has long been recognized not only in the literary field, but in the world of arts and cultural affairs.

In 1985, she was the recipient of the Noble Title of Dame of Magistral Grace from Dom Waldemar Baroni Santos, prince of Brazil, for her literary merits. In 1972, she was awarded the National Prize for Theatre in Brazil.

Pereira has been a member of the Academia Norteamericana de la Lengua Española and a correspondent of the Royal Spanish Academy since 1989. She is a member of the governing board of the World Congress of Poets and the research board of advisers of the American Biographical Institute. She is president of the International Writers and Artists Association, which she founded in the 1970s.

Her poetry and essays have been translated into more than twenty languages in over four hundred international journals. Pereira teaches Spanish and Hispanic American literature at Bluffton College in Ohio.

🐌 CECILE PINEDA

Born in New York City, Pineda grew up in a truly multilingual home. Her Mexican father, a professor at City College, spoke nine languages; her Swiss mother was fluent in several, as well as in the language of music. Pineda herself has a "reasonable command" of several European languages, including Serbo-Croatian and Polish. She is widely read and widely traveled, including tours for the U.S. Information Agency, and her fiction reflects a cosmopolitan grasp of the world. Prior to beginning her career as a novelist, Pineda founded and directed the experimental theater company Theater of Man in San Francisco. She is the author of the novel *Face* (1984), which won the Sue Kaufman Prize for First Fiction from the American Academy and Institute of Arts and Letters and a gold medal from the Commonwealth Club of California, and was nominated for a National Book Award. Pineda's second novel, *Frieze* (1985), was inspired by a trip to Borobudur, a ninth-century Buddhist shrine at Yogjakarta. The book chronicles the rise and fall of a civilization, "seen" through the eyes of an ultimately blind protagonist. Pineda's third novel is *The Love Queen of the Amazon* (1993), a picaresque novel which satirizes magical realism and takes to task some of that genre's major exponents.

Pineda's poetry is less well known, but she has been working on a collection entitled "Winding the Thread" for the last several years. Pineda is currently visiting writer at San Diego State University.

🐌 PINA PIPINO

Originally from Argentina, Pina Pipino holds a M.F.A. from Montclair State University. Her poems have appeared in *Perception III*,

Neon Literary Review, The Best New Voices in Poetry, ICON, and other literary magazines. Pipino's poem, "There Were Other Willows," received a Special Honorary Mention by the Theater Guild of New Jersey in 1993.

Pipino works for "a large law firm" in New Jersey. She is currently finishing a novel about the military depredations during the 1970s in Argentina.

🐌 NICOLE POLLENTIER

Of Mexican and German descent, Nicole Pollentier was the youngest contributor in *Daughters of the Fifth Sun: A Collection of U.S. Latina Fiction and Poetry* (Putnam, 1995). Her poetry was also included in *This Promiscuous Light* (Wings Press, 1996). She has been writing and publishing poetry most of her life, and was included in several issues of the respected *Young Pegasus* anthology. She was a staff editor of her high school literary magazine, which won national recognition from Columbia University. Her poetry has appeared in three issues of *Hanging Loose* and in several literary magazines, and received prizes from Palo Alto College, San Antonio, and from the C. W. Miller Poetry Contest, Trinity University. Pollentier is an accomplished folksinger, veteran coffeehouse poet, and a world traveler. She recently transferred from Brown University to the University of Texas at Austin, where she is pursuing an undergraduate degree in English.

🐌 BEATRIZ RIVERA

Born in Havana, Cuba, and raised in Miami, Beatriz Rivera has lived in Switzerland and France, where she obtained her master's degree from the University of Paris IV—Sorbonne. Since 1979, she has lived in and around New York City, working as a manuscript reader, a translator, an advertising copy writer, a university press editor, and a language teacher. Rivera is the author of *African Passions* (Arte Público Press, 1995), a collection of short fiction. Her first novel, *Terra Firma,* was published in 1997. Currently Rivera is finishing her Ph.D. from the University of Paris.

❧ Eliana Suárez Rivero

Born in Artemisa, Cuba, Eliana Suárez Rivero has lived in the United States since 1967. In 1968, she obtained her Ph.D. at the University of Miami, Florida. She is a noted scholar of contemporary Hispanic American poetry, particularly the work of Pablo Neruda. Currently she is a professor of Spanish literature at the University of Arizona in Tucson.

Two of her books, *El gran amor de Pablo Neruda: estudio crítico de su poesía/The Great Love of Pablo Neruda: A Critical Study of His Poetry* (1971) and *De cal y arena / Of Lime and Sand* (1975), were published in Spain. Her poetry has been included in numerous anthologies and magazines and in her own collection, *Cuerpos breves/Brief Bodies* (Arizona, 1976). She co-edited *Siete poetas/Seven Poets* (with Margarita Cota-Cárdenas (1978) and *Infinite Divisions: An Anthology of Chicana Literature* (with Tey Diana Rebolledo, 1994). Suárez Rivero is currently working on a study of U.S. Latino literature and a collection of autobiographical essays.

❧ Catherine Rodríguez-Nieto

Translator Catherine Rodríguez-Nieto has worked closely with poet Lucha Corpi for several years, having translated both of Corpi's books of poetry. She holds a M.A. in Spanish from the University of California at Berkeley. Her translations have appeared in numerous literary magazines, anthologies, and textbooks. Rodríguez-Nieto and her husband operate In Other Words, Inc., a translation and editing business in Oakland, California.

❧ Carmen Giménez Roselló

Born in New York City and raised in California, Giménez Roselló is currently a teaching fellow at the University of Iowa Writer's Workshop, where she is pursuing her MFA. Giménez Roselló's work has appeared in *Kalliope, Galley Sail Review, Reed Magazine,* and elsewhere. A short story was included in *New Voices: Young Latino Writers* (Bantam, 1996).

恓 BEVERLY SÁNCHEZ-PADILLA

A native of New Mexico, Beverly Sánchez-Padilla is an interdisciplinary artist, film and video producer, performance poet, and playwright. A postgraduate fellow of Massachusetts Institute of Technology, she is the author of five locally produced plays and the producer/director of several videos, including *El corrido de Juan Chacón* and *De mujer a mujer*. Currently she teaches creative writing and classes in television and film production for the San Antonio Independent School District.

恓 RAQUEL VALLE SENTÍES

A native of Laredo, Texas, Raquel Valle Sentíes is an award-winning photographer as well as being an actress, poet, and dramatist. After twenty years in Vera Cruz, she returned to Laredo and began writing. She received third place in the 1990 National Chicano Literary Contest (University of California at Irvine) for her play *Alcanzando un Sueño*. In 1995, El Teatro de la Esperanza in San Francisco performed her play *La Mala Onda de Johnny Rivera*.

Sentíes's poetry has appeared in various literary magazines. Her first collection, *Soy Como Soy y Qué* (M&A Editions, 1996) is an evocative exploration of *la vida en la frontera*.

恓 CARMEN TAFOLLA

Called a "world-class writer" by Alex Haley, Carmen Tafolla has published many books, the latest being *Sonnets to Human Beings*, which includes not only the title selection (which won the University of California at Irvine's 1989 National Chicano Literature Contest), but a large selection of Tafolla's poems and short stories, as well as many essays on Tafolla and her work. Tafolla's poems and short stories are included in many anthologies and in dozens of textbooks, at every level from elementary through college.

Tafolla was born in San Antonio, and her earlier poems employ the bilingual idiom of the city's west side. She has long been regarded as one of the masters of poetic code switching. *Curandera* (1983) is considered something of a core document in this regard.

In the 1970s, Tafolla was the head writer for *Sonrisas*, a pioneering bilingual television show for children. Her dramatic talents make her readings both lively and touching.

A scholar of note, Tafolla is the author of *To Split a Human: Mitos, Machos y la Mujer Chicana*. Tafolla has been a professor of women's studies at the University of California at Fresno, and special assistant to the president of Northern Arizona University. A much-sought-after educational consultant, she currently lives in McAllen, Texas, where she is working on a novel in between speaking engagements.

🐌 SHEILA ORTIZ TAYLOR

Florida State University professor Sheila Ortiz Taylor is a novelist and short story writer. She is the author of three novels, including *Faultline* (Naiad Press, 1982), a mosaic-like novel of contrasting narrative voices. Her subsequent novels, *Spring Forward/Fall Back* (Naiad, 1985) and *Southbound* (Naiad, 1990), established Taylor as a writer to watch.

Taylor is the author of one volume of poetry, *Slow Dancing at Miss Polly's* (Naiad, 1989), and her latest work is a memoir entitled *Imaginary Parents* (University of New Mexico Press, 1996).

🐌 GINA VALDÉS

Born in Los Angeles, California, Gina Valdés grew up on both sides of the U.S./Mexico border. Her work has been published in journals and anthologies in the United States, Mexico, and Europe. She is the author of two collections of poetry, *Comiendo lumbre/Eating Fire* (Maize Press, 1986) and *Puentes y fronteras/Bridges and Borders* (Bilingual Review Press, 1996).

🐌 GLORIA VANDO

Gloria Vando's long-awaited first collection of poetry, *Promesas: Geography of the Impossible* (1993), was preceded by many appearances in some of the top U.S. literary magazines. *Promesas* won the 1994 Thorp Menn Award for Poetry.

Vando earned her B.A. at Texas A & I, Corpus Christi, and attended New York University, the University of Amsterdam, and the Académie Julian in Paris. In 1991 Vando won the Billee Murray

Denny Poetry Prize. Other awards include the Kansas Fellowship in Poetry (the first granted by the state), a CCLM Editors Grant, and the Barbara Deming Memorial Award.

The poetry of Vando was described as "a universal voice expressing childhood anguish and passion" by *Publishers Weekly*, but this description does not convey the intellectual depth and historical content of her work.

Vando is founder-editor of *The Helicon Nine Reader,* an anthology featuring the best of *Helicon Nine,* which won the 1991 Governor's Arts Award (Kansas). She is also co-founder of the Writers Place, a literary resource center for writers and readers. She presently lives in Kansas City, where she publishes Helicon Nine Editions.

🐌 ENEDINA CÁSAREZ VÁSQUEZ

Enedina Cásarez Vásquez, an artist, poet, playwright, and short story writer, is the author of the collection *Recuerdos de una niña* (Centro de Comunicación Misioneros Oblatos de María, 1980) and such plays as *Te Traigo Estas Flores y Marshmallow Peeps, The Visit,* and *La Virgen de San Juan de los Lagos.* She is a founding member of the performance/writing group Mujeres Grandes and a noted folk artist, whose iconographic nichos are included in the permanent collections of several major museums, including the Smithsonian Institution. A lifelong resident of San Antonio, she was until recently an artist-in-residence with the San Antonio Independent School District. Currently she teaches art in a Catholic school.

🐌 EVANGELINA VIGIL-PIÑON

Shortly after winning the Coordinating Council of Literary Magazines' national poetry contest in 1976 for her strident feminist poem, "Ay qué ritmo," Vigil-Piñon published her first chapbook of poems. A masterly documentation of the bilingual idiom of the barrios of westside San Antonio, the language of *nade y nade* was praised for its "rich and varied simplicity." *Thirty an' Seen a Lot* (1982), written in the same idiom, received an American Book Award from the Before Columbus Foundation. Other awards and fellowships followed, including a poetry fellowship from the National Endowment for the

Arts and, most recently, recognition by the National Association of Chicano Studies for her work.

Vigil-Piñon is also the author of *The Computer Is Down* (1987), and the editor of the important (and pioneering) anthology of Latina writing, *Woman of Her Word*. She translated into English Tomás Rivera's classic novel, . . . *And the Earth Did Not Devour Him* (1992), now in its third edition.

☙ ALMA LUZ VILLANUEVA

Born and raised in the San Francisco Mission District, Alma Luz Villanueva is of Yaqui, Spanish, and German ancestry. Her first book of poetry, *Bloodroot* (1977), attracted considerable critical attention. That same year, her manuscript entitled simply "Poems" won the Third Chicano Literary Prize at the University of California at Irvine.

Villanueva's autobiographical poem, "Mother, May I?" (1978), which was long her best-known work, fictionalizes through personalized myth the cyclic changes in a woman's life and the joyous emergence into wholeness.

Her first novel, *The Ultraviolet Sky* (1988), was the recipient of the American Book Award of the Before Columbus Foundation. It has been reissued by Anchor Doubleday. Her second novel, *Naked Ladies*, was published in 1994.

Other poetry collections include *La Chingada* (1985), an epic poem published in English and Spanish, *Life Span* (1984), and *Planet* (1993). *Planet*, which won the Latin American Writers Institute Award in poetry (1994, New York), spotlights such issues as racism, sexual abuse, and poverty. Her latest book is *Weeping Woman: La Llorona and Other Stories* (1994).

Villanueva, who holds a MFA in writing, teaches creative writing at the University of California, Santa Cruz.

☙ BERNICE ZAMORA

Bernice Zamora is a respected and prolific poet and the author of many literary articles and reviews, short stories, critical essays, and monologues. Her work as an educator is of equal importance. Her fondest wish is to create a literature for Chicano youth, which will allow them "to feel a part of the world."

Restless Serpents (1976), her first book of poetry, was a collaborative collection of poems written with the late José Antonio Burciaga, which received national attention. *Releasing Serpents*, her second collection of poetry, was published in 1994. Her poems have appeared in numerous magazines and anthologies in the Americas and in Europe.

In 1979, Zamora became co-editor (along with José Armas) of *De Colores Journal*. In 1980, they co-edited an anthology resulting from the Flor y Canto festivals IV and V, held in Albuquerque (1977) and Tempe (1978).

Bernice Zamora received her Ph.D. in English and American studies from Stanford University in 1986. Zamora teaches literature and writing at Santa Clara University.

CREDITS AND PUBLICATION HISTORIES

The following selections are published by arrangement with their respective authors, unless otherwise indicated:

Teresa Palomo Acosta: "The corn tortilla," "In the season of change," "Today the pomegranate tree was in bloom," and "It is an exquisite fading away, I think" are published for the first time in this volume.

Marjorie Agosín: "Marta Alvarado, profesora de historia," "Marta Alvarado, History Professor," "Umiliana Cárdenas: pescadora de poetas," "Umiliana Cárdenas: Fisher-Poet," "El credo de Titania," and "Titania's Creed" are published for the first time in this volume.

Julia Alvarez: "Homecoming" was first published in *The Massachusetts Review* (no. 4, 1995). "The Dashboard Virgencita," "Dusting," and "Audition" are reprinted from *Homecoming* by Julia Alvarez (Plume, 1996). Copyright © Julia Alvarez, 1984, 1996. Used by permission of Susan Bergholz Literary Services, New York. All rights reserved.

Gloria Anzaldúa: "*Cihuatlyotl*, Woman Alone," "The Cannibal's *Canción*," and "La Curandera" are reprinted from *Borderlands/La Frontera: The New Mestiza* by Gloria Anzaldúa, Aunt Lute Books, 1987. © 1987 by Gloria Anzaldúa. By permission of the publisher.

Miriam Bornstein: "Una pequeña contribución" and "To a Linguist Studying Discourse Strategies of Bilingual/Bicultural Students" are published for the first time in this volume.

Giannina Braschi, translation by Tess O'Dwyer: "¡Las cosas que les pasan a los hombres en Nueva York!" and "The Things That Happen to Men in New York!" are reprinted from *Empire of Dreams* by Giannina Braschi (Yale University Press, 1994). By permission of the author and the publisher.

Norma E. Cantú: "Trojan Horse" and "Decolonizing the Mind" are published for the first time in this volume.

Ana Castillo: "You Are Real as Earth, y Más" appeared in *Berkeley Poetry Review* (no. 25, 1991–92). "Ixtacihuatl Died in Vain," "Someone Told Me," and "In My Country" are reprinted from *My Father Was a Toltec* by Ana Castillo (Norton, 1995). Used by permission of Susan Bergholz Literary Services, New York. All rights reserved.

Rosemary Catacalos: An early version of "A Silk Blouse" was published in *The Women's Review of Books* (Autumn 1994) and "At Home in the World" in *The Texas Observer* (1997). "Morning Geography" appeared in *Colorado Review* and later in *Paper Dance: Fifty-five Latino Poets*, edited by Victor H. Cruz et al. (Persea Books, 1995). "Insufficient Light" is published for the first time in this volume.

Lorna Dee Cervantes: "Beneath the Shadow of the Freeway" first appeared in *Latin American Literary Review* and reprinted in *Emplumada* by Lorna Dee Cervantes (University of Pittsburgh Press, 1981). By permission of the author and *Latin American Literary Review*. "On Love and Hunger" and "Lápiz Azul" are reprinted from *From the Cables of Genocide: Poems on Love and Hunger* by Lorna Dee Cervantes, Arte Público Press, 1991. By permission of the publisher. "Emplumada" is reprinted from *Emplumada* by Lorna Dee Cervantes. © 1981 by Lorna Dee Cervantes. Reprinted by permission of the University of Pittsburgh Press. "Bird Ave" appeared in *Chicana Creativity and Criticism,* edited by María Herrera-Sobek and Helena Viramontes (University of New Mexico Press, 1996).

Lisa Chávez: "The Crow's Bride" is published for the first time in this volume. "Wild Horses" was first published in *Calyx: A Journal of Art and Literature by Women* (Summer 1990).

Sandra Cisneros: "You Bring Out the Mexican in Me," "With Lorenzo at the Center of the Universe, el Zócalo, Mexico City," and "Once Again I Prove the Theory of Relativity" are reprinted from *Loose*

Palabra nueva: Poesía chicana edited by Ricardo Aguilar et al. (Dos Pasos Editores); and "Beggar on the Córdoba Bridge" in *Imagine: International Chicano Poetry Journal*. All were reprinted in *Three Times a Woman* by Alicia Gaspar de Alba, María Herrera-Sobek, and Demetria Martínez (Bilingual Press/Editorial Bilingue, 1989).

Celeste Guzmán: "La tía que nunca come azúcar" is published for the first time in this volume. "La cama de esperanza" was first published in *This Promiscuous Light: Young Women Poets of San Antonio*, edited by Bryce Milligan (Wings Press, 1996).

Sheila Sánchez Hatch: "Coatlícue" and "The Burning God" first appeared in *RiverSedge* (Fall 1992) and reprinted in *Linking Roots: Writing by Six Women with Distinct Ethnic Heritages*, edited by Bryce Milligan (M & A Editions, 1993). "Notes on Why Misogyny Is an Art Form" is published for the first time in this volume.

Maya Islas: "Viaje de una mujer sola" and "One Woman's Journey" are published for the first time in this volume.

María Limón: "cuando se habla de nombres" is published for the first time in this volume.

Rita Magdaleno: "Night Flight" and "The Leaving" are published for the first time in this volume.

Demetria Martínez: "To Keep Back the Cold" and "Nativity: For Two Salvadoran Women, 1986–1987" appeared in *Three Times a Woman* by Alicia Gaspar de Alba, María Herrera-Sobek, and Demetria Martínez (Bilingual Press/Editorial Bilingue, 1989).

Pat Mora: "La Buena Pastora," copyright © 1997 by Pat Mora. Published by agreement with Russell & Volkening as agents for the author. "Sonrisas" and "Bilingual Christmas" are reprinted from *Borders* by Pat Mora, Arte Público Press/University of Houston, 1986. By permission of the publisher. "Curandera" is reprinted from *Chants* by Pat Mora, Arte Público Press/University of Houston, 1985. By permission of the publisher. "La Migra" is reprinted from *Agua Santa: Holy Water* by Pat Mora. © 1995 by Pat Mora. Reprinted by permission of Beacon Press, Boston.

Elvia Padilla: "The border, she is a woman," "Woman as a River," and "Leave Her for Me" are published for the first time in this volume.

Anabella Paiz: "Moon Phases" is published for the first time in this volume.

Deborah Parédez: "A Cartography of Passions" is published for the first time in this volume. "Converging Boundary" first appeared in *This Promiscuous Light: Young Women Poets of San Antonio*, edited by Bryce Milligan (Wings Press, 1996).

Teresinka Pereira: "Alabanza al gusano" and "Poem to Praise Worms" are published for the first time in this volume.

Cecile Pineda: An earlier version of "On Seeing Vermeer's Geographer" appeared in *Fourteen Hills* (Spring 1996). "Blue Madonna" is published for the first time in this volume.

Pina Pipino: "White Scarves" and "Aliens" are published for the first time in this volume.

Nicole Pollentier: "Keeper of the Word" and "Always Fishing" are published for the first time in this volume.

Beatriz Rivera: "Lament of the Terrorist" is published for the first time in this volume.

Eliana Suárez Rivero: "Three for Two" and "History Revisited: In Québec, with a Friend" are published for the first time in this volume.

Carmen Giménez Roselló: "Frida" and "Plaza de Armas, Lima" are published for the first time in this volume.

Beverly Sánchez-Padilla: "Mali" first appeared in *La Voz de Esperanza* (Spring 1993).

Raquel Valle Sentíes: "Laredo" was first published in *Soy Como Soy y Que* (M & A Editions, 1996).

Carmen Tafolla: "New Song" first appeared in *Canto al Pueblo IV* (Mesa, Arizona, 1980). "Porfiria" first appeared in *Puerto del Sol* (vol. 22, no. 1, 1992) and reprinted in *Sonnets to Human Beings and Other Selected Works* by Carmen Tafolla (Lalo Press: Santa Monica, 1992). "La Malinche" first appeared in *Tejidos* (vol. 4, no. 4, 1977) and reprinted in *Five Poets of Aztlán* (Bilingual Review Press, 1985). "Mujeres del rebozo rojo" is published for the first time in this volume.

Sheila Ortiz Taylor: "Marker" and "The Way Back" are reprinted from *Slow Dancing at Miss Polly's* by Sheila Ortiz Taylor (Naiad Press, 1989).

Gina Valdés: "Spells" is published for the first time in this volume. "The Hands" is reprinted from *Eating Fire* by Gina Valdés (Maize Press, 1986).

Gloria Vando: "Los Alamos," "Cante Jondo," and "Promesas" are reprinted from *Promesas: Geography of the Impossible* by Gloria Vando, Arte Público Press, 1993. By permission of the publisher. "In the Crevices of Night" first appeared in *Cottonwood* (Summer 1994, Gloria Vando issue).

Enedina Cásarez Vásquez: "Bad Hair" first appeared in *Mujeres Grandes Anthology II*, edited by Angela de Hoyos (M & A Editions, 1995).

Evangelina Vigil-Piñon: "apprenticeship" and "la hondo" were first published in *Nade y nade* (M & A Editions, 1978). "Corazón en la palma," "the hands of time," and "crimson the color" are published for the first time in this volume.

Alma Luz Villanueva: "Even the Eagles Must Gather" was first published in *A Formal Feeling Comes: Poems in Form by Contemporary Women* edited by Annie Finch (Story Press, 1994). "Delicious Death" was published in *Paper Dance: Fifty-five Latino Poets*, edited by Victor H. Cruz et al. (Persea Books, 1995). "Warrior in the Sand" is published for the first time in this volume.

Bernice Zamora: "Contraries" and "Glint" are published for the first time in this volume.

FOR THE BEST IN PAPERBACKS, LOOK FOR THE

In every corner of the world, on every subject under the sun, Penguin represents quality and variety—the very best in publishing today.

For complete information about books available from Penguin—including Puffins, Penguin Classics, and Arkana—and how to order them, write to us at the appropriate address below. Please note that for copyright reasons the selection of books varies from country to country.

In the United Kingdom: Please write to *Dept. JC, Penguin Books Ltd, FREEPOST, West Drayton, Middlesex UB7 0BR.*

If you have any difficulty in obtaining a title, please send your order with the correct money, plus ten percent for postage and packaging, to *P.O. Box No. 11, West Drayton, Middlesex UB7 0BR*

In the United States: Please write to *Consumer Sales, Penguin USA, P.O. Box 999, Dept. 17109, Bergenfield, New Jersey 07621-0120.* VISA and MasterCard holders call 1-800-253-6476 to order all Penguin titles

In Canada: Please write to *Penguin Books Canada Ltd, 10 Alcorn Avenue, Suite 300, Toronto, Ontario M4V 3B2*

In Australia: Please write to *Penguin Books Australia Ltd, P.O. Box 257, Ringwood, Victoria 3134*

In New Zealand: Please write to *Penguin Books (NZ) Ltd, Private Bag 102902, North Shore Mail Centre, Auckland 10*

In India: Please write to *Penguin Books India Pvt Ltd, 706 Eros Apartments, 56 Nehru Place, New Delhi 110 019*

In the Netherlands: Please write to *Penguin Books Netherlands bv, Postbus 3507, NL-1001 AH Amsterdam*

In Germany: Please write to *Penguin Books Deutschland GmbH, Metzlerstrasse 26, 60594 Frankfurt am Main*

In Spain: Please write to *Penguin Books S. A., Bravo Murillo 19, 1° B, 28015 Madrid*

In Italy: Please write to *Penguin Italia s.r.l., Via Felice Casati 20, I-20124 Milano*

In France: Please write to *Penguin France S. A., 17 rue Lejeune, F−31000 Toulouse*

In Japan: Please write to *Penguin Books Japan, Ishikiribashi Building, 2−5−4, Suido, Bunkyo-ku, Tokyo 112*

In Greece: Please write to *Penguin Hellas Ltd, Dimocritou 3, GR−106 71 Athens*

In South Africa: Please write to *Longman Penguin Southern Africa (Pty) Ltd, Private Bag X08, Bertsham 2013*